The
Catholic
Youth Prayer
Book

Second Edition

Mary Shrader, Lauré L. Krupp,
Robert Feduccia Jr.,
and Matthew J. Miller

saint mary's press

Nihil Obstat: Rev. Timothy J. Hall, STL
 Censor Librorum
 December 20, 2012

Imprimatur: † Most Rev. John M. Quinn
 Bishop of Winona
 December 20, 2012

The nihil obstat and imprimatur are official declarations that a book or pamphlet is free of doctrinal or moral error. No implication is contained therein that those who have granted the nihil obstat or imprimatur agree with the contents, opinions, or statements expressed, nor do they assume any legal responsibility associated with publication.

The second edition publishing team included Gloria Shahin, editorial director, and Brian Singer-Towns, editor. Prepress and manufacturing coordinated by the production departments of Saint Mary's Press.

Printed in China

1365 (PO6280)

ISBN 978-1-59982-333-1, leatherette

Contents

Introduction

Why We Pray

I asked God for strength, that I might achieve;
I was made weak, that I might learn humbly to obey.
I asked for health, that I might do great things;
I was given sickness, that I might do better things.
I asked for riches, that I might be happy;
I was given poverty, that I might be wise.
I asked for power, that I might have the praise of men;
I was given weakness, that I might feel the need for God.
I asked for all things, that I might enjoy life;
I was given life, that I might enjoy all things.
I received nothing I asked for—but everything I hoped for.
Almost despite myself, my unspoken prayer was answered;
I am, among all men, most richly blessed.

—UNKNOWN CONFEDERATE SOLDIER

When we talk with God and ask for help, we are in conversation with the one being who has the power to do or change anything. God even has the power to change us.

Sometimes, we ask for God's guidance in a certain way and then find out we have grown differently. Placing our needs and concerns before God allows us to share the struggle with someone loving and accepting—and powerful.

In the process, not only do we find that a situation or problem is better than we thought, but also we are able to see the situation from a new perspective. This is the power and grace of God at work.

When we are able to focus ourselves in prayer, we gain new insights and new perspective and are humbled to embrace God's will in our lives.

Sometimes, in the thick of struggling times, we might feel sorry for ourselves. We might ask God for things that may not really be good for us. For example, "God, please make _____ love me" might be the prayer of a heartbroken person.

Psalm 139:13 tells us that God knew us before we were born. God knows everything about us. Because we do not know all that God knows, it is possible that we don't always ask for what is best—especially if we ask out of pity or selfishness.

Even though our plans might not turn out as we prayed, God surprises us with a wonderful alternative. For example, many young people have prayed to get into a college they had their hearts set on. When they received their rejection letters, they might have thought there was no hope for a good college experience. However, God may have opened a door for them to get into a different school, one that was perfect for them. Their years there were great, and they discovered a major that suited them perfectly.

All of this is part of the wonder of prayer. The most important part of prayer, the goal of prayer, is for us to be shaped in the image of Jesus. Through prayer we can be changed into the image of Jesus to love what he loved as deeply as he loved.

As the Son of God, Jesus knew and experienced the Father intimately. The experience of God as Father is offered to us in prayer. Jesus was love and gave everything he had for others. The process of being changed into love is ours in prayer. God loves us profoundly and wants to give us things. God wants us to ask. God also offers something more for us in prayer. God offers a relationship that fulfills the deepest longing of the human heart.

Imagine it, believe it, and then—*pray!* Pray when you are

- reflecting
- contemplating

- asking or petitioning
- sorrowing
- thankful or grateful
- joyful and praising
- searching or seeking

How to Use This Book

Although prayer is personal in many ways, it is also a community experience. When you pray, God hears you. In addition, all the angels and saints are praying for you and your prayer. Family, friends, and other people you know are united with you in prayer too. Therefore, prayer is ever changing, ever growing, ever evolving.

Because of the community aspect of prayer, some prayers have been handed down for many generations. These traditional prayers may have their origins in Scripture, the life of a saint, or a Catholic teaching or other specific person or event.

This book contains a collection of prayers. It includes some traditional prayers for you to pray. It also includes some contemporary and traditional ways to pray, such as an adaptation of the form of prayer known as the Liturgy of the Hours, and journal writing. These options offer you variety in the way you choose to pray. The way you choose to pray might depend on your mood, needs, and energy level.

This book's table of contents gives an overview of the prayers and prayer forms in this book. In addition to the prayers in each chapter, you will also find sidebar notes called Study It!, Pray It!, and Live It!

Study It!

Prayer has a deep history in our Catholic faith and is a rich part of our Tradition. The Study It! sidebar notes help you learn about prayer in general or describe the origins of certain prayers.

Pray It!

Look for ways to be inspired in your own prayer life. Maybe you will discover new ways to pray either individually or with your family, friends, and community.

Live It!

Read about the prayer lives of the saints. People's stories can help us learn more about the value of prayer and can inspire us to live a prayerful life focused on God's will for us. Listen to the lives of others. Think about how you incorporate prayer into your own life. If you have so much as uttered the words "But I don't know how to pray," then you are already on the way to learning how to pray. At the very least, prayer is talking to God, and there is no right or wrong way to do that. This book will introduce you to many great ways to pray. Just ask God to guide you, and God will plant the seeds of deeper prayer in your heart.

Tips

Think about how you like to pray. Is there someplace or something that inspires you to live a prayerful life? Create a prayer space, a prayer box, or a prayer journal that contains the information and tools you need to allow yourself the opportunity to pray often.

Consider having more than one of some of these items so you can easily invite a friend, parent, or sibling to pray with you.

- *The Catholic Youth Bible*® or another edition of the Bible
- a pen and paper for writing prayers and thoughts
- a cross or crucifix
- a rosary
- a candle
- matches or a lighter (Remember to practice fire safety!)
- prayer cards

- pictures of saints or family members who inspire you
- a prayer shawl or blanket
- a rug or mat
- a small table with a tablecloth
- holy water
- statues or icons of saints
- a small fountain (for the sound of water)
- a chair or other special place to sit or kneel
- flowers or other items from nature
- this book, other books, and resources that include prayers and writings that inspire you personally
- music (a CD and a CD player or musical instrument)
- art supplies, such as markers, paints, clay, chalk, and paper
- a special item, such as your own baptismal candle or a grandparent's rosary
- a missalette or other publication that lists the weekly readings

Your Comments or Suggestions

Saint Mary's Press wants to know your reactions to the materials in this book. We are open to all kinds of suggestions from young people and want to continue to provide resources that enliven your hearts and minds with the Good News of Jesus Christ. Please let us know how we can help you pray all ways.

If you have a comment or suggestion, please write to us at 702 Terrace Heights, Winona, MN 55987-1320, or send an e-mail to *smpress@smp.org*.

Part I

PRAYERS FOR DAILY LIFE

1 Prayers through the Day

Morning Prayers

Hymn for Sunday Morning: *"Te Deum"* ("You Are God")

You are God: we praise you;
You are the Lord: we acclaim you;
You are the eternal Father:
All creation worships you.
To you all angels, all the powers
 of heaven,
Cherubim and Seraphim, sing
 in endless praise:
 Holy, holy, holy, Lord, God of
 power and might, heaven and
 earth are full of your glory.
The glorious company of apostles
 praise you.
The noble fellowship of prophets
 praise you.
The white-robed army of martyrs
 praise you.
Throughout the world the holy
 Church acclaims you:
 Father, of majesty unbounded,
 your true and only Son,

worthy of all worship,
 and the Holy Spirit, advocate
 and guide.
You, Christ, are the king of glory,
the eternal Son of the Father.
When you became man to set
 us free
you did not spurn the Virgin's
 womb.
You overcame the sting of death,
and opened the kingdom of
 heaven to all believers.
You are seated at God's right
 hand in glory.
We believe that you will come,
 and be our judge.
Come then, Lord, and help
 your people,
bought with the price of your
 own blood,
and bring us with your saints
to glory everlasting.

Ignatian Examination of Conscience

Saint Ignatius of Loyola wanted to be fully present to God throughout his day. To prepare for the next day, he reviewed the day he had just lived. This review, or examination, brought to mind ways he was present to God and ways he needed to be more present to God.

Before you go to bed at night, take a little time to end your day with God. This will help you let go of the day and start tomorrow fresh—a clean slate, a new beginning. Following are several ways to do so:

- Begin by thanking God for the day.
- Ask the Holy Spirit to help you see the day through his eyes.
- Think through your day, hour by hour. Getting out of bed and ready for school . . . arriving at school and seeing your friends . . . going through your morning classes . . . lunch . . . afternoon classes . . . after-school activities . . . coming home . . .
- What are you grateful for? When did you see God working? For those moments, pray, "Thank you, God, for . . ."
- What are you sorry for? Everyone sins. The greatest damage, however, isn't in the moment of the act itself but is in the effects the act has on others, ourselves, and our relationship with God. We can feel shameful, or we may think we are bad people. It is much better simply to acknowledge our sins and shortcomings and to ask God and others to forgive us.
- After you have contemplated your day, ask God to help you grow closer to him.
- Last, ask God to guard you while you sleep, to keep your heart and mind fixed on him, and to help you wake up ready to serve throughout another day.

Psalm 33:20–22

Our soul waits for the Lord;
 he is our help and shield.
For in him our hearts rejoice;
 in his holy name we trust.
May your mercy, LORD, be
 upon us;
 as we put our hope in you.

Take This Day

To Jesus, who changed the water
 into wine:
Take this day
and make it into something
 beautiful.
Amen.

A True Friend to Jesus

To Jesus, who called us friends:
Let me be a true friend to
 you today.
Let my words and my actions
tell the world how much
 I love you.
Amen.

The Morning Offering

O Jesus,
through the Immaculate Heart
 of Mary,
I offer You my prayers, works,
 joys, and sufferings
of this day for all the intentions
 of Your Sacred Heart,
in union with the Holy Sacrifice
 of the Mass
throughout the world,
in reparation for my sins,
for the intentions of all my
 relatives and friends,
and in particular for the
 intentions of the Holy Father.
Amen.

Sanctifying the Day

To *sanctify* means to set something aside for holiness. Just how do you sanctify your day, or make it holy?

God makes things holy!

To set your day aside for God, simply recognize that you are in God's presence constantly. God is already there and is already aware of what is happening with you. Remember this. Turn to God and say yes.

The film *The Prince of Egypt* (1998, 90 minutes, rated PG) is the animated story of God's calling Moses to lead the Hebrews out of Egypt. At the burning bush, Moses draws near and hears God calling his name: "Moses! Moses!" Moses cannot see the person calling, but the voice becomes like a wind whirling around him. Moses finds himself lifted off his feet by the power of this call.

Think of God's presence in your life as being like that wind. It is constantly around us. God's presence and call to us are as real as the air we breathe. We cannot see air. Yet, though it is invisible, though it is most often forgotten, air is still real. It still gives us life.

In the middle of a busy day, remembering God can be hard. But God doesn't go away when we don't think about God. God is all around us, like the air we breathe.

Use a reminder that will help you remember to turn to God, perhaps every time the bell rings if you are at school. Pray: "Thank you, God, for being with me. Help me stay near you as I continue my day."

Connect your day with God. Make it, and yourself, holy.

Prayers at School

Prayer before a Test

Lord:

I have studied, but there is so
 much to remember.

Please give me a clear mind.

Please keep distractions away
 from me.

Do not allow the pressure of the
 moment to frustrate me.

Help me instead to calmly take
 this test with the confidence

that you will help me remember
 everything I have studied.

Amen.

Prayer after a Test

Lord:

I worry about my grades.

It is very easy for me to obsess
 over a test

I am going to take and tests
 I have taken.

I give you my concerns about
 the test I have just taken.

I ask that the teacher grade it fairly,

and I ask that I go about the
 rest of the day with confidence
 that I did my best.

Amen.

Prayer for Holy Words

Merciful Jesus:

It is very easy for me to join
 my friends

when someone is being talked
 about,

when the conversation is

about something inappropriate,

or when the language becomes
 coarse.

Give me the right words when

the wrong words are being used.

May my words be only those that
 will bless others,

not hurt or offend them.

Amen.

Saint Ignatius of Loyola

Saint Ignatius of Loyola is an inspiration to all who have been confused about what they should do with their life or what God calls them to, or perhaps to those who think they are following God but then get turned around.

Ignatius began life as, well, a partier. He was rich and popular and hung out at the royal court with all the other rich and popular people. But he was also a soldier. After being hit by a cannonball in battle, Ignatius was laid up for quite a while. The only books around were those about Christ and the lives of the saints. With nothing else to do, Ignatius began reading. These stories stirred his soul to the point that he committed himself to a life of faith and virtue.

Exactly what that meant, however, wasn't clear. Ignatius decided to travel to the Holy Land, which is modern-day Israel and surrounding areas. After a long and difficult journey, he arrived, only to be told he had to leave. He often suffered from poverty and bad health and was the victim of rumor campaigns.

Years after his injury, Ignatius gradually began to understand God's way. Eventually, Ignatius founded a religious order called the Society of Jesus, also known as the Jesuits. Ignatius centered the life of his order on a love for Jesus that was lived every moment of the day. He challenged the other Jesuits to become aware of God's calling in the small things. He instructed his followers to stop at moments through the day and to be aware of how they were saying yes to God.

Live It!

Prayers at Meals

Prayer before Meals
Bless us, O Lord, and these
your gifts, which we are about
to receive from your bounty,
through Christ, our Lord.
Amen.

Prayer after Meals
We give you thanks for all your
benefits almighty God,
who lives and reigns forever
and ever.
Amen.

Prayers at Midday

Psalm 19:15
Let the words of my mouth
be acceptable,
the thoughts of my heart
before you,
LORD, my rock and
my redeemer.

Psalm 23
The LORD is my shepherd;
there is nothing I lack.
In green pastures he makes me
lie down;
to still waters he leads me;
he restores my soul.
He guides me along right paths
for the sake of his name.
Even though I walk through
the valley of the shadow
of death,
I will fear no evil, for you are
with me;

your rod and your staff
comfort me.
You set a table before me
in front of my enemies;
You anoint my head with oil;
my cup overflows.
Indeed, goodness and mercy will
pursue me
all the days of my life;
I will dwell in the house of
the LORD
for endless days.

You Are Near
Lord:
Keep me mindful of your love,
and help me remember that you
are near.
Amen.

Night Prayers

Night Prayer Antiphon

Protect us, Lord, as we stay
 awake;
watch over us as we sleep,
that awake, we may keep watch
 with Christ, and asleep,
rest in his peace.
Amen.

Psalm 141:1–4

LORD, I call to you; hasten to me;
 listen to my plea when I call.
Let my prayer be incense
 before you;
 my uplifted hands an evening
 offering.
Set a guard, LORD, before my
 mouth,
 keep watch over the door of
 my lips.
Do not let my heart incline
 to evil,
 to perform deeds in
 wickedness.
On the delicacies of evildoers
 let me not feast.

Canticle of Simeon: Luke 2:29–32

Now, Master, you may let your
 servant go
 in peace, according to
 your word,
for my eyes have seen your
 salvation,
 which you prepared in sight
 of all the peoples,
a light for revelation to the
 Gentiles,
 and glory for your people
 Israel."

While I Sleep

Lord God:
I know that you can be at work,
even while I sleep.
Keep my heart and mind on you.
Heal me of injury,
make my heart strong,
make my soul pure,
and may I grow closer to you.
Amen.

2 Prayers for Life Events

A Simple Prayer

O God,
Open my ears to hear you
and my heart to receive you,
and strengthen my will
that I may follow you.
Amen.

God Is Light

Loving God:
Take away the darkness
and fill me with the radiant light
of your Son, Jesus Christ.
Amen.

I Have Faith

Jesus Christ, my Lord:
I can't explain it, Lord,
but today I know you are
 with me.
I know you hold me
in the palm of your hand.
I know you love me
and will guide me.
I know there is nothing
you can't do.

I know there is nothing
you won't do
for me.
Amen.

It's a Great Day

God of glory:
Thank you, God,
for all you have given me,
for everything that makes today
 great—
the tangible things
and this good feeling I have
but can't explain.
Amen.

It's a Jungle Out There, God

Lord, I hate to watch the news.
Sometimes I feel
as though the world is spinning
out of control.
I know that you haven't
abandoned us,
but sometimes
I wonder where you are.
Then I remember

Joyful Hearts, Give Praise!

What does praising God mean? We know how to thank God. We know how to ask God for things. We know how to ask God to forgive us. We know how to pray. But what does it mean to praise God?

Giving thanks is about acknowledging what God does; giving praise is about acknowledging who God is. The root of the word *praise* also gives us the word *prize*. What do you prize about God?

Who is God? How have you experienced God? Some like to think of God's loving nature. Others like to think of God as a friend who never leaves their side. You may prize God's constancy. No matter how many things change in your life, God remains the same. What do you love about God?

Make a list of things you prize about God. This list is your own litany of praise. Read your list and make it your prayer. Before each thing you prize, say, "I praise you, God, for . . ." This will become your praise, your gift to God.

that I am your hands, your feet.
It is my voice
through which you speak.
Let me remember
that I may not be able to change
the whole world,
but I may be able to
make all the difference
in the world of one person.
Amen.

There Is So Much

Lord Jesus, who calmed the
 stormy sea:
There is so much pressure,
there is so much hurt,
there is so much confusion,
there is so much noise.
Jesus, please calm this storm,
so that I may
sit peacefully in this boat
 with you.
Amen.

I Can't Do Anything Right

God:
It feels like I can't do anything
 right,
like I woke up in a parallel
 universe or something.
Help me to remember today that
 wherever I am,
you are there,

and that your love for me doesn't
 depend on what I do.
You love me just because I am.
Amen.

Why Did You Let It Happen, God?

I don't get it,
and I don't get you.
Why did you let it happen?
I don't understand.
But even though I am mad at you,
I still feel hope inside me.
I trust you,
even though I don't know why.
I guess that deep down I know
you will help me through.
I choose to believe in you
in the middle of it all.
Amen.

Confused

Jesus, light of the world
and light of my world too:
No matter how dark the
 darkness is,
your light is shining.
Help me to keep my eyes on
 your light
and not on the darkness that
 swarms around me.
I don't know what your plan for
 me is, Lord,

but I know you have one.
Help me to hang on
until the time is right
for you to show it to me.
Amen.

My Dream Is Shattered

Loving God,
who cares about my dreams:
Bless and restore me.
In my disappointment
 and sadness,
help me to remember
that you have a future full of
 hope for me.
Give me a new dream.
Amen.

I'm Sorry, God

Jesus, you forgave Peter
for denying you three times.
Please give me the guts
to be honest with myself.
Give me the humility
to admit my sins.
And give me wisdom
so I will know how to repair the
 harm I have caused.
Forgive me, Lord,
for what I have done,
and give me the grace
not to do it again.
Amen.

Boyfriend or Girlfriend Trouble

Jesus, you promised to carry
 my burdens:
I have a broken heart,
and I have to live with it
while I deal with homework,
friends,
and everything else.
Lord Jesus,
will you carry my heavy heart?
Will your love fill the empty
 space
that was left when love was taken
 from me?
Amen.

My Family

Jesus,
son of Mary and Joseph,
I love my family, Lord.
And I want what's best for them.
I wish I knew how to say that
 to them.
Help me, Jesus, to find the
 words.
But while I am looking,
will you hear my prayer for them,
and bless them,
and let them know that you
 love them?
Amen.

Growing Closer to God

When we think of growing, we usually think of an upward movement. Plants become taller when they grow. A promotion at work means a step up on the ladder.

Growing closer to God is all about going deeper, not moving up.

"I will place my law within them, and write it upon their hearts; I will be their God, and they shall be my people" (Jeremiah 31:33). To grow closer to God, we must go to the depth of our hearts, where God's Law is written, where God dwells. We don't have to add something new to our hearts; rather, we must learn to listen to that place in our hearts where God's Law is already written. The more we listen, the easier hearing God becomes.

"Baptism seals the Christian with the indelible spiritual mark (*character*) of his belonging to Christ"[1] (*Catechism of the Catholic Church*, 1272).

You were forever changed when you were baptized. When the mark of Jesus Christ was engraved onto your soul, you received a homing device of sorts that leads you back to God—if you listen.

Think of sunflowers. They are unusual by almost any measure. They are taller, stronger, and bigger than most flowers. Of course, the most fascinating aspect of sunflowers is that they follow the sun as it makes its way across the sky. They do this even on cloudy days. Somehow, they just do it.

As sunflowers follow the sun, so does your heart follow God—unless we weaken ourselves through sin. Sin separates us from God and causes us to become weak and less than God intended. The key is to avoid sin and to listen to your heart—to go to the depths where God's Word is written, where the mark of your Baptism is found. There you will learn to grow strong in virtue to be the beautiful person God created you to be!

Study It!

Thank You for My Friend

Thank you, Jesus,
for sending my friend
to speak with me.
Thank you for reminding me
that you are thinking of me,
and thank you for my friend.
Amen.

My Friend Is Hurting

Jesus,
you cared about your friends:
My friend is hurting, Lord,
and I don't know how to help.
Bless [name], Lord,
and give comfort, healing,
 and peace.
Amen.

Mother Teresa

Saint Cecilia

Imagine walking through an underground tunnel, a seemingly endless maze of small rooms and nooks. It is damp and cold, and despite the lamps, you cannot help but feel the darkness of the place.

Your thoughts turn to the people who first dug these tunnels, called catacombs. The diggers were the Christians during the time that Christianity was illegal in Rome, a time when being a Christian could get a person killed. The Christians of those days hid in these tunnels for meetings, for celebrating the Eucharist, and for fellowship.

You come to a room a bit larger than the others. There you see a sculpture of Saint Cecilia that was created ages ago. The room is filled with vibrantly colored murals of her. Everything about this room says Cecilia was unique.

Cecilia was a noblewoman of her time who gave up everything for her faith. After the Roman authorities martyred her husband and his brother for their Christian faith, Cecilia brought their bodies to her estate and buried them there. For this the authorities sentenced Cecilia to die. She lived for three days after an executioner attempted to behead her. During that time, Cecilia used her worldly goods to take care of people who were poor, made provisions to leave her home to the Christian Church, and continued to sing praises to God. That is part of the reason she is the patron saint of singers. Even through the painful wounds of an executioner, Cecilia gave praise.

In the pains and sufferings of life, Cecilia can inspire us always to have a joyful heart that is focused on the Lord.

Live It!

Left Out by Friends

Jesus, on the Cross:
You know what hurt is
and how it feels
to be left behind by your friends.
You know how I feel,
and I know how you felt.
I will stay with you today,
and I know that you will stay
 with me.
Amen.

Living True

Jesus:
Sometimes I know exactly what
 you want me to do,
but I don't have the courage to
 do it.
I am tired of being this way.
Help me to stand up straight
and be who you made me
 to be—
Strong, confident, and unafraid.
Amen.

I Want to Do Good Work in the World

Lord,
you call me to great things.
You have created me good.
In my Baptism, you placed
 within me
the same Spirit

that raised Christ Jesus from
 the dead.
Help me, Lord,
to open my heart
and let the good that you have
 placed in me
flow out into the world.
Amen.

The Path I Want to Walk

Loving God,
the Bible says
that your Word is a lamp for
 my feet
and a light for my path.
Light my way, God,
while I fill out college
 applications
and choose my major
and interview for jobs.
Help me to find the path
that you have laid out for me.
Amen.

Waiting for "the One"

I am lonely, Lord,
waiting,
waiting for "the one"
to come into my life.
Be with me, Jesus,
and help me to have hope,
because right now
I feel sad and alone.

Help me to trust in your plan
and to have faith that you
 will provide
all that I need.
Amen.

Jesus, I Trust You

Jesus, you fed the multitudes:
Help me to have the courage
of the boy who brought you
the five loaves and two fish.
With your blessing,
his small gift
became enough to feed five
 thousand.
Let me never think of myself
as not quite enough.
You have blessed me,
and with you,
I have everything I need.
Amen.

You Are with Me

Jesus, you said, "I am with
 you always":
Help me to keep my heart open
 today, Lord,
so I can feel your love at work
 in me.
You are always present to me,
 Lord.
Today let me be present to you.
Amen.

3 Opening and Closing Prayers

This chapter contains short prayer services for eight common group situations. There is a prayer to be used at the beginning and at the end of each situation. Each prayer has parts for a leader and a reader. The readings are from Scripture and could be read from the Bible.

Prayers for Class

Prayer to Begin Class

All: +In the name of the Father . . .

Leader: Let us recall that we are in the holy presence of God.

(Pause for a moment of silence.)

Reader: After they had completed [the days of Passover], as they were returning, the boy Jesus remained behind in Jerusalem, but his parents did not know it. Thinking that he was in the caravan, they journeyed for a day and looked for him among their relatives and acquaintances, but not finding him, they returned to Jerusalem to look for him. After three days they found him in the temple, sitting in the midst of the teachers, listening to them and asking them questions, and all who heard him were astounded at his understanding and his answers.

(LUKE 2:43–47)

Leader: Lord of all wisdom, open our minds and hearts to your truth. Help us learn what we need to learn. Give us the grace to do more than we think we can do today. We ask this through Christ our Lord.

All: Amen.

Prayer to End Class

Leader: Let us recall that the Lord our God is in our midst.

(Pause for a moment of silence.)

Reader: The spirit of the Lord GOD is upon me, / because the LORD has anointed me.

(ISAIAH 61:1)

Leader: Holy God, let us live more fully in your Spirit, that we might walk in confidence. Let us go forth from today certain that with your Spirit upon us, we are empowered to do more than we think we can do. We ask this through Christ our Lord.

All: Amen. +In the name of the Father . . .

Prayers for Team Practice

Prayer before Practice

All: +In the name of the Father . . .

Leader: Let us recall that we are in the holy presence of God.

(Pause for a moment of silence.)

Reader: They that hope in the LORD will renew their strength, / they will soar on eagles' wings; / they will run and not grow weary, / walk and not grow faint.

(ISAIAH 40:31)

Leader: All-giving God, we thank you for the abilities you have given us and for bringing us together today. We ask you to bring this group of individuals together into a powerful team. Help us to do our best, and help us to trust others to do their best. Keep us safe from injury, and help us stay focused on our goals. We ask this through Christ our Lord.

All: Amen.

Prayer after Practice

Leader: Let us recall that the Lord our God is in our midst.

(Pause for a moment of silence.)

Reader: I have competed well; I have finished the race; I have kept the faith. From now on the crown of righteousness awaits me, which the Lord, the just judge, will award to me on that day, and not only to me, but to all who have longed for his appearance.

(2 TIMOTHY 4:7–8)

Leader: Thank you, Lord, for helping us today, for keeping us safe, and for helping us stay focused. As we leave this practice, we ask that you keep building this team, so that we can be an example to our classmates of what a group of people working toward a common goal can accomplish together. We ask this through Christ our Lord.

All: Amen. +In the name of the Father . . .

Prayers for a Meeting

Prayer to Begin a Meeting

All: +In the name of the Father . . .

Leader: Let us recall that we are in the holy presence of God.

(Pause for a moment of silence.)

Reader: [And Jesus said,] "Everyone who listens to these words of mine and acts on them will be like a wise man who built his house on rock. The rain fell, the floods came, and the winds blew and buffeted the house. But it did not collapse; it had been set solidly on rock."

(MATTHEW 7:24–25)

Leader: Lord God, let our ears be attentive to your leading. Guide us with your holy wisdom. Let all that we do be built on you, our Rock. We ask this through Christ our Lord.

All: Amen.

Prayer to End a Meeting

Leader: Let us recall that the Lord our God is in our midst.

(Pause for a moment of silence.)

Reader: Let my prayer be incense before you, / my uplifted hands an evening offering.

(PSALM 141:2)

Leader: All-good God, we ask you to receive the work of our hands as a sign of our love for you. Bless what we have accomplished during this meeting. We all lead busy lives, Lord; help us to live out our best intentions. Give us the determination we need to complete the commitments that we have made here. We ask this through Christ our Lord.

All: Amen. +In the name of the Father . . .

Leading Others in Prayer

As a young person, you have perhaps never been invited to lead people in prayer before. How does one lead others in prayer?

To answer that question, let's look at what the Catholic bishops of the United States say to church musicians:

> The church musician is first a disciple and then a minister. . . . he or she is a worshiper above all. Like any member of the assembly, the pastoral musician needs to be a believer, needs to experience conversion, needs to hear the Gospel and so proclaim the praise of God. Thus, the pastoral musician is not merely an employee or volunteer. He or she is a minister, someone who shares faith, serves the community, and expresses the love of God and neighbor through music. (United States Conference of Catholic Bishops, *Liturgical Music Today*, 23)

Reread this passage, and replace the word *musician* with *leader* as you read. What advice does it offer you as a leader of prayer?

When you are called on to lead prayer, you will find some practical steps helpful: review the prayer service, practice reading the prayers aloud, read slowly and confidently, and look at people as you read. But remember also to reflect on this beautiful excerpt from the U.S. bishops to prepare your heart as well.

Pray It!

Prayers for a Service Project

Prayer before a Service Project

All: +In the name of the Father . . .

Leader: Let us recall that we are in the holy presence of God.

(Pause for a moment of silence.)

Reader: Whoever serves me must follow me, and where I am, there also will my servant be. The Father will honor whoever serves me.

(JOHN 12:26)

Leader: Good and gracious God, we thank you for gathering us here today and for giving us this opportunity to serve. May we be a witness to your love and your goodness to everyone we meet. Bless our work this day, and bless those we serve. We ask this through Christ our Lord.

All: Amen.

Prayer after a Service Project

Leader: Let us recall that the Lord our God is in our midst.

(Pause for a moment of silence.)

Reader: You are my friends if you do what I command you. I no longer call you slaves, because a slave does not know what his master is doing. I have called you friends, because I have told you everything I have heard from my Father.

(JOHN 15:14–15)

Leader: Loving God, thank you for calling us your friends. Thank you for this chance to be together, to serve together, and to live the Gospel together. As we leave here today, may we be more grateful for our blessings and be ready to share those blessing with others. We ask this through Christ our Lord.

All: Amen. +In the name of the Father . . .

What Is the Liturgy of the Hours?

Perhaps you have seen your priest carrying a small book with many ribbons. The book is used to pray the Liturgy of the Hours. The full Liturgy of the Hours is commonly a four-volume set, but some people pray with excerpts collected in a single volume.

Liturgy of the Hours (also called the Divine Office) is the official public, daily prayer of the Catholic Church. The Divine Office provides standard prayers, Scripture readings, and reflections at regular hours throughout the day, including Morning Prayer, Daytime Prayer (midmorning, midday, or midafternoon), Evening Prayer (late afternoon or early evening), and Night Prayer (right before bed).

Ordained clergy are required to pray the Divine Office every day, as are the members of many religious institutes. However, anyone can pray the Liturgy of the Hours, and the Church encourages laypeople to make it part of their own daily prayer life. In fact, many parishes are starting to include the Liturgy of the Hours as part of the parish prayer. You may see notices in your bulletin that say, "Morning and Evening Prayer will be held at . . ." Stop by and pray sometime. Don't worry if you don't know what to do—people will assist you. You will find that it feels very much like the Liturgy of the Word at Sunday's Mass.

The *Catechism of the Catholic Church* explains: "This celebration, faithful to the apostolic exhortations to 'pray constantly,' is 'so devised that the whole course of the day and night is made holy by the praise of God' "[2] (1174). As you go about your day, take comfort and encouragement from knowing that so many people are praying and making the world holy.

Study It!

Prayers for a Youth Group Meeting

Prayer to Begin a Youth Group Meeting

All: +In the name of the Father . . .

Leader: Let us recall that we are in the holy presence of God.

(Pause for a moment of silence.)

Reader: The community of believers was of one heart and mind. . . . With great power the apostles bore witness to the resurrection of the Lord Jesus, and great favor was accorded them all.

(ACTS 4:32–33)

Leader: Father of us all, thank you for bringing us here. Thank you for the faith that unites us. Let us give each other the gift of a clean slate, so that we can be free of labels. Help us to create a safe place where each person feels free to be himself or herself. Help us, Lord, to share with one another honestly. We ask this through Christ our Lord.

All: Amen.

Prayer to End a Youth Group Meeting

Leader: Let us recall that the Lord our God is in our midst.

(Pause for a moment of silence.)

Reader: How good and how pleasant it is, / when brothers [and sisters] dwell together as one!

(PSALM 133:1)

Leader: Good and loving God, thank you for being with us and among us. Thank you for the honesty here. We ask you for the grace to continue standing with one another when we return to our schools and our families. May this unity that we experience here give us the strength to cope with stresses we face in our lives. Bless us, Lord, and bless all those we love. We ask this through Christ our Lord.

All: Amen. +In the name of the Father . . .

Prayers for a Retreat Team

Prayer before Leading a Retreat

All: +In the name of the Father . . .

Leader: Let us recall that we are in the holy presence of God.

(Pause for a moment of silence.)

Reader: But how can they call on him in whom they have not believed? And how can they believe in him of whom they have not heard? And how can they hear without someone to preach?

(ROMANS 10:14)

Leader: Give us the words, Lord, to share your Good News with the people who will be on retreat with us. Help us share your hope, your light, and your love. Bless the speakers as they share, the musicians as they sing and play, and all others who work on this retreat. Lead us, Lord, so that we can lead those who will attend this retreat. We ask this through Christ our Lord.

All: Amen.

Prayer after Leading a Retreat

Leader: Let us recall that the Lord our God is in our midst.

(Pause for a moment of silence.)

Reader: I give thanks to my God at every remembrance of you, praying always with joy in my every prayer for all of you, because of your partnership for the gospel from the first day until now. I am confident of this, that the one who began a good work in you will continue to complete it until the day of Christ Jesus.

(PHILIPPIANS 1:3–6)

Leader: God who keeps promises, we thank you for being with us for this retreat. We pray that as everyone returns home to their families, they will know of your love for them in a deeper way. We leave them in your hands, Lord, and we ask that you will complete the good work that you have begun. We ask this through Christ our Lord.

All: Amen. +In the name of the Father . . .

The School Chapel

A simple sign at the door read "Chapel." The interior was dusty and smelly, with old sheet music scattered on the chairs and floor, with dingy windows and dead plants. The chapel appeared abandoned. A small door off to the side opened into the sacristy, which was being used as a storeroom.

The chaplain rallied his friends, and the great cleanup began. The chapel and sacristy were clean and ready by the students' arrival that fall.

The chaplain began celebrating morning Mass. Only one or two students came in those first weeks. But as the weeks rolled into months, students responded to the invitation to come to Mass, and they began to extend an invitation to their friends and classmates. At some point in the second year, Mass attendance flowed into the hall outside the chapel. The students developed a tradition of signing large cards to send to members of their community, saying, "We prayed for you at Mass today." People who were homebound, struggling families, students going through a hard time, total strangers—the cards were treasured by those who received them.

Students graduated. New students came and entered the chapel and its tradition. As the years continued, the chaplain began receiving letters and e-mails from his former students. They had taken what they found in their school chapel to their universities, to their jobs, to their children, to the priesthood. Soldiers took it to the battlefields. The chaplain realized that the little chapel where his students had come to pray had expanded far beyond the walls of the school. It had become a chapel they carried in their hearts.

Prayers for a Dance

Prayer before a Dance

All: +In the name of the Father . . .

Leader: Let us recall that we are in the holy presence of God.

(Pause for a moment of silence.)

Reader: All you peoples, clap your hands; / shout to God with joyful cries.

(Psalm 47:2)

Leader: God of all goodness, thank you for gathering us here for this dance. Thank you for our friends, the music, and the chance to be together to have a good time. Let us welcome you among us tonight, and welcome your presence in one another. We ask this through Christ our Lord.

All: Amen.

Prayer after a Dance

Leader: Let us recall that the Lord our God is in our midst.

(Pause for a moment of silence.)

Reader: Rejoice in the Lord always. I shall say it again: rejoice! Your kindness should be known to all. The Lord is near.

(Philippians 4:4–5)

Leader: God our joy, thank you for the good time we enjoyed here. Thank you for everyone who worked to make this dance possible. We ask your blessing on them. As we leave this place and drive home, we ask you to keep us safe. Give us the grace to be grateful always for the things we have, especially for the people in our lives who care about us. We ask this through Christ our Lord.

All: Amen. +In the name of the Father . . .

© Saint Mary's Press / Vicki Shuck, Illustrator

The Shofar

Prayers for a Graduation Party

Prayer to Begin a Graduation Party

All: +In the name of the Father . . .

Leader: Let us recall that we are in the holy presence of God.

(Pause for a moment of silence.)

Reader: Go, eat your bread with joy and drink your wine with a merry heart, because it is now that God favors your works.

(Ecclesiastes 9:7)

Leader: Good and loving God, thank you for this gathering to celebrate the graduation of [name]. Thank you for his or her family, friends, teachers, coaches, and everyone who helped [name] get to this moment. Give [name] the grace to open up his or her heart to enjoy this celebration and to fully express gratitude to all who come to this party. We ask this through Christ our Lord.

All: Amen.

Prayer to End a Graduation Party

Leader: Let us recall that the Lord our God is in our midst.

(Pause for a moment of silence.)

Reader: For I know well the plans I have in mind for you . . . plans for your welfare and not for woe, so as to give you a future of hope. When you call me, and come and pray to me, I will listen to you.

(Jeremiah 29:11–12)

Leader: God of the journey, thank you for this party and its reminder of the people who are important to us. Thank you for the past years and for what [name] has accomplished. Thank you, too, for the hardships, because we know that hardships are part of what makes us into who we are. Help [name] to accept the blessings with gratitude, to reconcile where reconciliation is needed, and to move forward, confident in your plan for her or his life. We ask this through Christ our Lord.

All: Amen. +In the name of the Father . . .

4 Blessing Prayers

Blessing for a New School Year

O Lord of wisdom,
You who know the innermost
 secrets of the universe,
send us your Paraclete
and cause us to grow in wisdom,
knowledge, and understanding.
When it is time to work,
give us the grace to stay focused.
When we participate in a
 competition,
give us the grace to show good
 sportsmanship.
When it is time to enjoy,
give us the grace to help us set
 concerns aside.
Above all, O Lord,
let us grow closer to you.
We ask these things
through Jesus Christ our Lord.
Amen.

Blessing before an Entrance Exam

All-powerful God,
you who created our inmost
 being:
Send us your Holy Spirit.
In your kindness, help us to
 stay focused
during this exam.
Help us call to mind those things
 we know,
which may be hidden behind
 clouds of anxiety.
Give us the grace
to put forth our best effort
and then leave the results in
 your hands.
We make this prayer
through Christ our Lord,
who reigns with you
forever and ever.
Amen.

Pray It!

Intercessory Prayer

"I'll pray for you." How many times have you said that to someone? How many times did you actually pray for that person? Sometimes it seems as though "I'll pray for you" is what we say when we don't know what to say. Yet because we are a blessed and holy people, our prayers do much to move the heart of God.

Here's something to try. Keep a small journal by your bed. Each night, write down what you promised to pray for that day, and how you promised to pray for it. Then look through your journal, and let your list guide your prayer. If you find a prayer that has been answered, don't cross it off your list. Turn your "Please, God" into a "Thank you, God!"

How can we pray when we don't know what to say? Saint Paul tells us, "In the same way, the Spirit too comes to the aid of our weakness; for we do not know how to pray as we ought, but the Spirit itself intercedes with inexpressible groanings" (Romans 8:26). When you don't know what to pray, close your eyes and try to see the person in your mind. As you look at the person, say, "Be with [name], Lord; be with [name]." Keep looking at the person for a moment in your mind's eye, and then pray it again . . . and then again. Let the Spirit of God pray for you.

Blessing before an Awards Banquet

All-powerful God,
you who separated the night and
 the day,
the water and the dry land:
We come to you this day
grateful for all we have
 accomplished together.
Grant that we who have enjoyed
 triumphs
will be good stewards of the gifts
 you have given us.
May our success give glory
 to God,
the giver of all good things.
We make this prayer
in the all-powerful name
of Jesus Christ our Lord.
Amen.

Blessing for One Going on a Mission Trip

God our protector,
you stand guard over our
 comings and goings:
Watch over our [brother/sister], N.,
as [he/she] goes forth from
 our midst
to serve you.
Keep [name] safe from all harm,
and keep [his/her] heart open to
 receive your grace.

Comfort N. if [he/she] feels
 homesick,
and bring [him/her] new friends
 to share this journey.
We ask this through your Son,
 Jesus Christ,
who reigns with you
forever and ever.
Amen.

Blessing for Those Going on a Pilgrimage

All-powerful God,
you always show mercy toward
 those who love you
and you are never far away for
 those who seek you.
Remain with your servants on
 this holy pilgrimage
and guide their way in accord
 with your will.
Shelter them with your
 protection by day,
give them the light of your grace
 by night,
and, as their companion on
 the journey,
bring them to their destination
 in safety.
We ask this through Christ
 our Lord.
Amen.

—From *Book of Blessings*, 603

Blessed and Holy

The first blessing appears in the very first chapter of the Bible—Genesis, chapter 1. Grab your Bible and take a look. You will find that first blessing on the fifth day of Creation, when God created and blessed the first living beings, all his creatures (v. 21). Then on the sixth day, after God created man and woman, God blessed them (v. 28).

To bless is to make holy. And what is holy? That which is joined to God. In other words—you.

At your Baptism the priest anointed you with the Chrism of salvation so that you would remain forever a member of Christ who is Priest, Prophet, and King. You are joined with God. Therefore you are holy.

Although we can be uncomfortable with the word *holy*, it is important to recognize that we are blessed and holy by virtue of our creation in God's image and of our Baptism. So when you pray that your loved one will be "blessed," he or she will be blessed, because of the prayers of a holy person. Pray with confidence, for God hears the prayers of those who are joined to him.

Blessing for One Leaving for the Military

Lord God,
Father to all children,
you have counted,
each hair on our head:
We ask you now to watch
 over N.,
your [daughter/son].
Give N. the grace
to carry the knowledge of your
 love and care
with [her/him]
wherever military service takes
 [her/him].
We pray that you keep all soldiers
 from harm.
Keep special watch over those in
 hostile places,
and return them safely to their
 families and friends.
We make this prayer through
Jesus Christ, our Lord,
who reigns with you
forever and ever.
Amen.

Blessing for One Celebrating a Birthday

God of all creation,
We offer you grateful praise for
 the gift of life.
Hear the prayers of N.,
 your servant,
who recalls today the day of his/
 her birth and rejoices in your
 gifts of life and love,
family and friends.
Bless him/her with your presence
and surround him/her with
 your love
that he/she may enjoy many
 happy years,
all of them pleasing to you.
We ask this through Christ
 our Lord.
Amen.

—From *Book of Blessings*, 343

Blessing for One Celebrating an Engagement

We praise you, Lord,
for your gentle plan draws
 together your children,
N. and N.,
in love for one another.
Strengthen their hearts,
so that they will keep faith with
 each other,
please you in all things,
and so come to the happiness of
 celebrating the sacrament
of their marriage.
We ask this through Christ
 our Lord.
Amen.

—From *Book of Blessings*, 211

Commissioning of Leaders in the Early Church

Blessing at a Gravesite

Almighty God and Father,
by the mystery of the cross, you
 have made us strong;
by the sacrament of the
 resurrection you have sealed us
 as your own.
Look kindly upon your servants,
now freed from the bonds of
 mortality,
and count them among your
 saints in heaven.
We ask this through Christ
 our Lord.
Amen.

—From *Book of Blessings*, 1749

Blessing of a Pet

O God,
the author and giver of every gift,
animals also are part of the way
 you provide help
for our needs and labors.
We pray (through the
 intercession of Saint N.)
that you will make available for
 our use
the things we need to maintain a
 decent human life.
We ask this through Christ
 our Lord.
Amen.

—From *Book of Blessings*, 957

The Radical Example of Saint Clare

You have probably heard of Saint Clare. At seventeen years old, Clare heard Saint Francis of Assisi preach, and she decided that she wanted to live as Francis did.

Beautiful and rich, Clare could have lived any life she wanted. What did she want? To give her wealth to the poor, leave her beautiful home, and live a cloistered life of poverty and prayer with other women.

Just another teenager? No, she was much more than that. Today young women still follow Clare's example. They have radically given up their possessions and their connections with family and friends to join the Poor Clares, a cloistered community of women who pray for the world.

In a letter to Pope John Paul II, Mother Mary Francis—an abbess of the Poor Clare Monastery of Our Lady of Guadalupe in New Mexico—explained that her community steps away from the world, but not apart from the world. It is in following this radical call that a Poor Clare can give herself completely to God and to prayer for the world.

The prayers of these holy women bless the world. But you don't need to join the Poor Clares to pray for the world. Look at your schedule. Can you find five minutes a day to step *away* from the world so you can pray *for* the world?

Live It!

Blessing of a Planting

Lord of the harvest,
you placed the gifts of creation in
 our hands
and called us to till the earth and
 make it fruitful.
We ask your blessing
as we prepare to place these seeds
 (seedlings) in the earth.
May the care we show these seeds
 (seedlings)
remind us of your tender love for
 your people.
We ask this through Christ
 our Lord.
Amen.

—From *Book of Blessings*, 1021

Blessing of a Harvest

All-powerful God,
we appeal to your tender care
that even as you temper the
 winds and rains
to nurture the fruits of the earth
you will also send upon them
the gentle shower of your
 blessing.
Fill the hearts of your people
 with gratitude,
that from the earth's fertility
the hungry may be filled with
 good things
and the poor and needy proclaim

the glory of your name.
We ask this through Christ
 our Lord.
Amen.

—From *Book of Blessings*, 1021

Blessing of an Advent Wreath

Lord God,
let your blessing come upon us
as we light the candles of this
 wreath.
May the wreath and its light
be a sign of Christ's promise to
 bring us salvation.
May he come quickly and not
 delay.
We ask this through Christ
 our Lord.
Amen.

—From *Book of Blessings*, 1540

Part II

PRAYERS FROM
THE CATHOLIC TRADITION

5 Prayers and Devotions to Mary

Hail Mary

Hail Mary, full of grace,
the Lord is with you!
Blessed you are among women,
and blessed is the fruit of your
 womb, Jesus.
Holy Mary, Mother of God,
pray for us sinners
now and at the hour of
 our death.

The Oldest Marian Prayer: *"Sub Tuum Praesidium"* ("Under Your Protection")

We fly to your patronage,
 O Holy Mother of God.
 Despise not our petitions
 in our necessities but deliver
 us always from all dangers,
 O glorious and blessed Virgin.

The Angelus

The Angelus is traditionally recited morning (6:00 a.m.), noon, and evening (6:00 p.m.). Monks pray Morning Prayer, Midday Prayer, and Evening Prayer. By praying at set times of the day, the entire day is made holy. In the Middle Ages, the local churches' bells rang at these set times, and the laypeople stopped their work, gathered in small groups of two or more, and prayed the Angelus as a way to make their day holy. The Angelus can be said either in a group or alone.

Leader: The Angel of the Lord declared unto Mary,

Response: And she conceived of the Holy Spirit.

All: Hail Mary . . .

Leader: Behold the handmaid of the Lord,

Response: Be it done unto me according to your word.

All: Hail Mary . . .

Leader: And the Word was made flesh,

Response: And dwelt among us.

All: Hail Mary . . .

Leader: Pray for us, O holy Mother of God,

Response: That we may be made worthy of the promises of Christ.

Leader: Let us pray: Pour forth, we beseech you, O Lord, your grace into our hearts that we to whom the incarnation of Christ, your Son, was made known by the message of an angel may, by his passion and Cross, be brought to the glory of his resurrection, through Christ our Lord.

Hail, Holy Queen

Hail, holy Queen, mother of mercy, our life, our sweetness, and our hope.

To you do we cry, poor banished children of Eve.

To you do we send up our sighs, mourning and weeping in this vale of tears.

Turn then, most gracious advocate,
your eyes of mercy toward us, and after this our exile show to us the blessed fruit of your womb, Jesus.

O clement, O loving,

O sweet Virgin Mary.

"Memorare" ("Remember, O Most Gracious Virgin Mary")

Remember, O most gracious Virgin Mary, that never was it known that anyone who fled to your protection, implored your help or sought your intercession was left unaided. Inspired with confidence, I fly to you, O virgin of virgins, my Mother. To you I come, before you I stand, sinful and sorrowful. O Mother of the Word Incarnate, despise not my petitions, but in your mercy, hear and answer me. Amen.

Beads and Mantras

Throughout the world's many religions, including Catholicism, *mantras* have an important place in prayer and meditation. A mantra is a word or phrase that one repeats while meditating. The repetition occupies the body and allows the mind and spirit to pray more completely. When praying the Rosary, the Hail Marys become a mantra.

Beads are also used in other world religions besides Catholicism. For example, Muslims use a set of ninety-nine beads. Each bead represents a name for God in the Islamic faith. These beads become a kind of mantra for the hands.

In praying the Rosary, the beads help one keep count of the Our Fathers and Hail Marys. But the beads also help the person engage the entire body in prayer. Through the repetition of the mantra and the handling of the beads, a person's body, mind, and spirit are active and can enter more deeply into the mysteries of Jesus' life.

Pray It!

"Novena to Our Lady of Perpetual Help"

A novena is a process of praying for nine consecutive periods of time (typically nine days in a row). If something particular is on someone's mind or heart, that person may seek the prayers of Our Lady of Perpetual Help by praying these prayers for nine days.

Give your loving gaze to me, Our Lady of Perpetual Help. I am a person who wants to follow your Son, Jesus, but find it difficult. I come to you for comfort and help.

O Mother of Mercy, come to my aid. I hear that you are called the refuge and the hope of sinners and the weak. Be my refuge and my hope.

Help me, for the love of Jesus Christ. Stretch out your hand to take me by the hand and guide me to your Son. I simply and humbly entrust myself to your prayers and help. I bless and thank Almighty God, who in God's mercy has given me this confidence in you.

Mary, tender Mother, help me. Mother of Perpetual Help, may I always keep my eyes on Jesus and follow him with all my heart. Amen.

Pray the Lord's Prayer, Hail Mary, and Glory Be, three times each.

Easter Hymn to Mary: *"Regina Coeli"* ("Queen of Heaven")

Queen of heaven, rejoice, alleluia.
The Son whom you merited to bear, alleluia,
has risen as he said, alleluia.
Rejoice and be glad, O Virgin Mary, alleluia!
For the Lord has truly risen, alleluia.

The Rosary

Twenty mysteries are reflected upon in the Rosary: five joyful mysteries, five luminous mysteries, five sorrowful mysteries, and five glorious mysteries. As suggested by Pope John Paul II, the joyful mysteries are said on Monday and Saturday, the luminous on Thursday, the sorrowful on Tuesday and Friday, and the glorious on Wednesday and Sunday (with these exceptions: on Sundays of the Christmas season, the joyful mysteries are prayed; and on Sundays of the Lenten season, the sorrowful mysteries are prayed).

Guide to Saying the Rosary

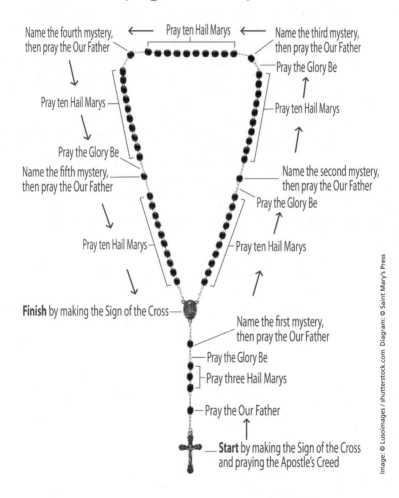

Name the fourth mystery, then pray the Our Father ← Pray ten Hail Marys ← Name the third mystery, then pray the Our Father

Pray the Glory Be

Pray ten Hail Marys

Pray ten Hail Marys

Pray the Glory Be

Pray the Glory Be

Name the fifth mystery, then pray the Our Father

Name the second mystery, then pray the Our Father

Pray the Glory Be

Pray ten Hail Marys

Pray ten Hail Marys

Finish by making the Sign of the Cross

Name the first mystery, then pray the Our Father

Pray the Glory Be

Pray three Hail Marys

Pray the Our Father

Start by making the Sign of the Cross and praying the Apostle's Creed

Image: © Lusoimages / shutterstock.com Diagram: © Saint Mary's Press

The History of the Rosary

The word *rosary* quickly calls to mind the image of roses. This is the actual origin of the word. The Rosary is seen as a bouquet of roses for Mary, the Mother of God. Although the origin of the word is easy to identify, the history is a bit more complex.

To understand the Rosary, the place of the Psalms should first be explained. The 150 Psalms constituted the prayer book of Jews, Jesus, and the early Christians. One group of these Christians was monks. With the Psalms as their prayer book, many communities of monks committed themselves to praying all of the Psalms within the span of a month, a week, or even a day. Before the introduction of the luminous mysteries in 2002, the entire Rosary consisted of 150 Hail Marys, just as there are 150 Psalms. By meditating on the life of Jesus and by praying 150 Hail Marys, the Christians who lived and worked in the world had a way to join the monks in their constant praise of God.

Study It!

The Joyful Mysteries

- The Annunciation: The Archangel Gabriel announces to Mary that she will be the mother of God's Son.
- The Visitation: While she is pregnant with Jesus, Mary visits her cousin, Elizabeth, who is pregnant with John the Baptist.
- The Nativity: Jesus, the Savior, is born.
- The Presentation: According to Jewish religious law, Jesus is brought to the Temple as an infant and dedicated to God.
- The Finding in the Temple: Mary and Joseph find Jesus in the Temple, instructing the elders after being lost.

The Luminous Mysteries

- The Baptism of the Lord: John the Baptist baptizes Jesus.
- The Wedding at Cana: At Mary's request, Jesus turns water into wine.
- The Proclamation of the Gospel: Jesus announces that he was sent to bring Good News—liberty and favor from the Lord.

The Transfiguration

- The Transfiguration: Peter, James, and John see Jesus transfigured. His face becomes as dazzlingly bright as the sun.
- The Institution of the Eucharist: Jesus shares with his Apostles the meal that perpetuates his earthly presence.

The Sorrowful Mysteries

- The Agony in the Garden: When faced with his death, Jesus is anguished to the point of his sweat becoming like drops of blood.
- The Scourging at the Pillar: After Jesus is arrested, he is beaten as though he were a criminal.
- The Crowning with Thorns: The soldiers mock Jesus as king by placing a thorny crown on his head.
- The Carrying of the Cross: Despite being weakened by abuse, Jesus carries his heavy Cross through the streets of Jerusalem.
- The Crucifixion: Jesus is nailed to the Cross and dies.

The Glorious Mysteries

- The Resurrection: Jesus rises from the dead!
- The Ascension: After rising from the dead, Jesus is taken up into Heaven to reign with the Father and the Holy Spirit.
- The Descent of the Holy Spirit: As he promised, Jesus sends the Holy Spirit upon Mary and the disciples to give them power to live as Christians.
- The Assumption of Mary: Mary is taken up into Heaven, body and soul, because she is sinless and lived her life in accordance with God's will for her.
- The Crowning of Mary as Queen of Heaven and Earth: The special role given to Mary on earth is continued in Heaven as she prays for all people to be faithful disciples of her son, Jesus.

Saint Louis de Montfort

Louis Mary Grignion de Montfort was born to a poor family on January 31, 1673, at Montfort, France, and was ordained to the priesthood in 1700.

Eventually Saint Louis went to Rome, where Pope Clement XI appointed him a missionary in a part of France known as Brittany. Louis was known for his impassioned preaching and his ability to draw people into a deep devotion to Mary. He also wrote a very popular book, *True Devotion to the Blessed Virgin*. In 1715 Louis organized several priests and formed the Missionaries of the Company of Mary. He died in 1716. In 1947 Pope Pius XII canonized him.

The spiritual legacy of Louis has had a lasting impact on the Church. In recent times, Pope John Paul II had a very deep love for Mary. In fact, at one point in his life, he wondered if his devotion to Mary was excessive. Was his love for Mary crowding out his love for Jesus? The Pope found his answer in the words of Louis. In *True Devotion to the Blessed Virgin*, the Holy Father found that his devotion was not excessive. Louis said that true devotion to the Blessed Mother always leads to a greater intimacy with the Lord Jesus.

Live It!

6 Prayers about the Holy Spirit

Come, Holy Spirit, Come

Come, Holy Spirit, come!
And from your celestial home
 Shed a ray of light divine!
Come, Father of the poor!
Come, source of all our store!
 Come, within our bosoms
 shine.
You, of comforters the best;
You, the soul's most welcome
 guest;
 Sweet refreshment here below;
In our labor, rest most sweet;
Grateful coolness in the heat;
 Solace in the midst of woe.
O most blessed Light divine,
Shine within these hearts
 of yours,
 And our inmost being fill!
Where you are not, we have
 naught,
Nothing good in deed or
 thought,
 Nothing free from taint of ill.
Heal our wounds, our strength
 renew;

On our dryness pour your dew;
 Wash the stains of guilt away:
Bend the stubborn heart and will;
Melt the frozen, warm the chill;
 Guide the steps that go astray.
On the faithful, who adore
And confess you, evermore
 In your sevenfold gift descend;
Give them virtue's sure reward;
Give them your salvation, Lord;
 Give them joys that never end.
 Amen.
 Alleluia.

—Pentecost Sequence from
the *Lectionary for Mass*

Prayer to the Holy Spirit

Come, Holy Spirit, fill the hearts
of your faithful. Enkindle in
them the fire of your love. Send
forth your Spirit and they will be
created. And you will renew the
face of the earth.

Lord, by the light of the Holy
Spirit, you have taught the hearts

of the faithful. In the same Spirit, help us to relish what is right and always rejoice in your consolation. We ask this through Christ our Lord. Amen.

Confirmation Consecratory Prayer

All-powerful God, Father of our
 Lord Jesus Christ,
by water and the Holy Spirit
you freed your sons and
 daughters from sin
and gave them new life.
Send your Holy Spirit upon them
To be their Helper and Guide.

Give them the spirit of wisdom
 and understanding,
the spirit of right judgment
 and courage,
the spirit of knowledge and
 reverence.
Fill them with the spirit of
 wonder and awe in your
 presence.
We ask this through Christ
 our Lord.
Amen.

—From *The Rites of the
Catholic Church*,
Rite of Confirmation, 42

Acts of the Apostles

© Saint Mary's Press / Vicki Shuck, illustrator

Pray It!

How Do I Pray to the Holy Spirit?

As a third person of the Holy Trinity, the Holy Spirit is as present to you as God the Father and God the Son.

Look at the Creation account in the first chapter of Genesis. Though all was "without form or shape," a "mighty wind" hovered over the waters (Genesis 1:2). Then look at Haggai 2:1–5, where God says, "My spirit remains in your midst; do not fear!" (v. 5), though destruction lies all around. Now turn to the account of the Annunciation in Luke 1:26–35. The angel tells Mary, "The holy Spirit will come upon you, and the power of the Most High will overshadow you" (v. 35).

These passages recount three very different scenarios, but they all show us that no matter what the circumstance, the Spirit of God was present—and that Spirit brought new life.

To pray to the Holy Spirit, begin by thinking of the Spirit of God as being as near to you as the air you breathe. As you sit quietly, breathe in and pray, "Come, Holy Spirit." As you breathe out, release your cares and worries into that presence. The Holy Spirit is always present to you. Prayer happens when we choose to be present to the Holy Spirit.

Prayer to the Holy Spirit

Breathe in me, O Holy Spirit, that
 my thoughts may all be holy.
Act in me, O Holy Spirit, that
 my work, too, may be holy.
Draw my heart, O Holy Spirit,
 that I love but what is holy.
Strengthen me, O Holy Spirit, to
 defend all that is holy.
Guard me, then, O Holy Spirit,
 that I always may be holy.
Amen.

—Prayer from Saint Augustine

Act of Consecration to the Holy Spirit

I pray to you, God the Holy
Spirit, and I give all of myself to
you. I worship you for you are
pure, just, and powerful as love.
You are my strength. You are my
guide. I ask for you to surround
me and change me. Change my
mind to think like Jesus. Change
my body to act like Jesus. Change
my heart to love like Jesus. Give
me the ears to hear your voice
guiding me, and when I hear your
voice, may I obey. Make me holy
and joyful. Give me the courage
I need to live as a missionary.
May people come to know Jesus
because I am in their lives. Amen.

Prayer for the Seven Gifts of the Holy Spirit

Christ Jesus, before ascending
into Heaven, you promised to
send the Holy Spirit to your
Apostles and disciples. Grant that
the same Spirit may perfect in
our lives the work of your grace
and love. Grant us:

- **The Spirit of Fear of the Lord** that we may be filled with a loving reverence toward you;
- **The Spirit of Piety** that we may find peace and fulfillment in the service of God while serving others;
- **The Spirit of Fortitude** that we may bear our cross with you and, with courage, overcome the obstacles that interfere with our salvation;
- **The Spirit of Knowledge** that we may know you and know ourselves and grow in holiness;
- **The Spirit of Understanding** to enlighten our minds with the light of your truth;
- **The Spirit of Counsel** that we may choose the surest way of doing your will, seeking first the Kingdom;

Scripture Tells Us about the Holy Spirit

What does it mean to say the Holy Spirit is at work in you? Learn about yourself through these passages from Scripture:

- You are brave! "For God did not give us a spirit of cowardice but rather of power and love and self-control" (2 Timothy 1:7).

- You are wise! "We speak . . . not with words taught by human wisdom, but with words taught by the Spirit, describing spiritual realities in spiritual terms" (1 Corinthians 2:13).

- You belong to a family! "For in one Spirit we were all baptized into one body, whether Jews or Greeks, slaves or free persons, and we were all given to drink of one Spirit" (1 Corinthians 12:13).

- You are strong! "If the Spirit of the one who raised Jesus from the dead dwells in you, the one who raised Christ from the dead will give life to your mortal bodies also, through his Spirit that dwells in you" (Romans 8:11).

- You will do great things! "It shall come to pass / I will pour out my spirit upon all flesh. / Your sons and daughters will prophesy, / your old men will dream dreams, / your young men will see visions" (Joel 3:1).

Study It!

- **The Spirit of Wisdom** that we may aspire to the things that last forever; Teach us to be your faithful disciples and animate us in every way with your Spirit.

Amen.

Grant Us Wisdom

O God, who have taught the
hearts of the faithful
by the light of the Holy Spirit,
grant that in the same Spirit we
may be truly wise
and ever rejoice in his
consolation.
Through our Lord Jesus Christ,
your Son,
who lives and reigns with you in
the unity of the Holy Spirit
one God, for ever and ever.
Amen.

—FROM *THE ROMAN MISSAL*,
VOTIVE MASS OF THE HOLY SPIRIT

Cleanse Our Thoughts

O God, to whom every heart
lies open,
every desire speaks plainly
and from whom no secret is
hidden,
cleanse, we pray, the thoughts of
our heart

by the outpouring of the
Holy Spirit,
that we may merit to love
you perfectly
and offer you worthy praise.
Through our Lord Jesus Christ,
your Son,
who lives and reigns with you in
the unity of the Holy Spirit,
one God, for ever and ever.
Amen.

—FROM *THE ROMAN MISSAL*,
VOTIVE MASS OF THE HOLY SPIRIT

Confirm Our Hearts

Grant, we pray, almighty God,
that the splendor of your glory
may shine forth upon us
and that, by the bright rays of the
Holy Spirit,
the light of your light may con-
firm the hearts
of those born again by your grace.
Through our Lord Jesus Christ,
your Son,
who lives and reigns with you in
the unity of the Holy Spirit,
one God, for ever and ever.
Amen.

—FROM *THE ROMAN MISSAL*, VIGIL
MASS FOR PENTECOST SUNDAY

Give the Spirit to Your People

God our Father,
you sent your Holy Spirit upon
 the apostles,
and through them and their
 successors
you give the Spirit to your people.

May his work begun at Pentecost
continue to grow in the hearts of
 all who believe.
We ask this through Christ our
 Lord.
Amen.

—From *The Rites of the Catholic Church*, Rite of Confirmation, 30

Novena to the Holy Spirit

Follow this course of prayer for nine days.

First Day: Creation Awaits Fulfillment

Holy Spirit, Lord of light!
 From your clear celestial
 height, your pure beaming
 radiance give!
Almighty and eternal God, send
 forth your Spirit, who brought
 order from chaos at the
 beginning of the universe, and
 peace to the Lord's disciples.
Grant that I, as your creation,
 baptized in your Spirit, may
 be filled with the seven gifts
 so that I may forever do your
 will and renew the face of
 the earth.
Amen.

Pray the Lord's Prayer, the Hail Mary, and the Glory Be.

Second Day: Christ's Promise to Send the Paraclete

Come, Father of the poor!
Come, treasures which endure!
Come, Light of all that live!
Come, O Blessed Spirit of Holy
 Fear, fill me with devotion to
 God alone.
In the Risen Christ, I welcome
 you, O Spirit of Truth, whom
 the Father sends in Jesus' name.
Wash clean the sinful soul,
 and rain down your grace
 that we may be one with the
 Church in fidelity to our
 Lord Jesus Christ.
Amen.

Pray the Lord's Prayer, the Hail Mary, and the Glory Be.

Third Day: The Soul of Christ's Body, the Church

You, of all consolers, best,
Visiting the troubled breast
Dost refreshing peace bestow.
Come, O Blessed Spirit of Piety,
 possess my heart.
God, our Father, may I, through
 the grace of your Spirit,
 be forever filled with filial
 affection for you.
Grant that I may be inspired to
 love and respect all members
 of your family as brothers and
 sisters of Jesus, who, together
 with him, call you Abba, Father.
Amen.

*Pray the Lord's Prayer, the Hail
Mary, and the Glory Be.*

Fourth Day: The Dignity of the Christian

Thou, in toil art comfort sweet;
Pleasant coolness in the heat;
Solace in the midst of woe.
Come, O Blessed Spirit of
 Fortitude, uphold my soul in
 time of trouble and adversity.
O, Divine Trinity, grant that we
 may be strengthened to see in
 ourselves and each other the
 dignity that is ours as temples
 of your Holy Spirit, to be

loved by one another as each
 of us is loved by Jesus.
We ask this through Christ our
 Lord.
Amen.

*Pray the Lord's Prayer, the Hail
Mary, and the Glory Be.*

Fifth Day: Gifted to Serve and Build Up Others

Light immortal! Light Divine!
Visit you these hearts of ours,
 And our inmost being fill!
Come, O Blessed Spirit of Know-
 ledge, and grant that I may
 perceive the will of the Father.
Father, through your Spirit,
 you invite us to participate
 in the fullness of Creation.
 Help me to see that all gifts
 are from you and intended for
 your Glory.
For there are many different
 gifts, but always the same
 Spirit, many ways of serving,
 but always the same Lord.
Amen.

*Pray the Lord's Prayer, the Hail
Mary, and the Glory Be.*

Sixth Day: Human Weakness and Sinfulness

If you take your grace away,
Nothing pure in man will stay,
All his good is turned to ill.
Come, O Blessed Spirit of
 Understanding, enlighten our
 minds that we may appreciate
 and see more fully what we
 know by faith.
Come to us in our weakness
 and give voice to our petitions,
 for "the prayers that the Spirit
 makes for God's holy people
 are always in accordance with
 the mind of God."
Amen.

*Pray the Lord's Prayer, the Hail
Mary, and the Glory Be.*

Seventh Day: Growth in the Freedom That Love Gives

Heal our wounds—our strength
 renew;
On our dryness, pour thy dew;
Wash the stains of guilt away!
Come, O Blessed Spirit of
 Counsel. Make my thoughts
 holy, my love pure, and my
 works pleasing to God.
Father, guided by your Spirit,
 may I strive to make loving
 choices and respect all life.

May we be aware of our
 dignity as your sons and
 daughters, redeemed with the
 Blood of your beloved Son,
 Jesus Christ our Lord.
Amen.

*Pray the Lord's Prayer, the Hail
Mary, and the Glory Be.*

Eighth Day: Gifted through the Spirit

Bend the stubborn heart and will;
Melt the frozen, warm the chill;
Guide the steps that go astray!
Come, O Blessed Spirit of
 Wisdom, strengthen my faith,
 increase my hope, perfect my
 charity.
Father, enlighten us each day,
 in the silence of our hearts,
 to discern the voice of your
 Spirit, to do what he asks of us
 and to understand the gifts he
 freely gives us.
We ask this through Christ our
 Lord.
Amen.

*Pray the Lord's Prayer, the Hail
Mary, and the Glory Be.*

Ninth Day: Sent with the Power to Reconcile

You on those who evermore,
you confess and you adore,
In your sevenfold gifts, descend;
Give them comfort when they die;
Give them life with you on high;
Give them joys that never end.
Father, through Jesus, your Son,
 you sent the Paraclete to be
 at our side, to reconcile all
 Creation to you.
Grant that I may be forever
 open to Jesus' invitation to
 "Receive the Holy Spirit!"
 Father, open our hearts to
 accept your forgiveness for
 our sins and to offer that same
 forgiveness to those who we
feel have offended us. For
 merciful forgiveness is the
 essence of your love revealed
 in your Son.
Come, O Divine Spirit, fill my
 heart with your heavenly
 fruits—your charity, joy,
 peace, patience, benignity,
 goodness, faith, mildness and
 temperance—that I may, by
 faithful submission to your
 inspiration, merit to be united
 eternally with you in the love
 of the Father and the Son.
Amen.

Pray the Lord's Prayer, the Hail Mary, and the Glory Be.

Saint Peter

Saint Peter was a man who couldn't quite seem to deliver. No one in his early life would have looked at him and said: "Hey, that guy will be the first Pope! He will help spread a new religion throughout the world!"

Throughout the Gospels, we see examples of Saint Peter's tendency to jump into something, only to pull back. He started to walk on water, but he got nervous and sank. He grabbed a sword and cut off the ear of the soldier arresting Jesus, but he denied knowing Jesus when he talked to another soldier, only hours later.

All that changed at Pentecost.

Immediately upon receiving the Holy Spirit, Saint Peter began to preach. He became bold, courageous. He no longer pulled back at the last minute—he continued forward.

In Acts of the Apostles, chapter 3—one chapter after the account of Pentecost—we see quite clearly that Peter is a new man. Saints Peter and John were going to the Temple to pray when they encountered a beggar. Surely the old Peter would have tried to help the beggar. But the passage in Acts says something interesting. It says that Peter looked intently at the man and then replied, "I have neither silver nor gold, but what I do have I give you: in the name of Jesus Christ the Nazorean, [rise and] walk" (3:6).

Saint Peter shows us that when we are empowered by the Holy Spirit, the best part of ourselves rises to new life.

Live It!

7 Prayers from the Saints

Only One Thing Is Necessary

O my God, help me to
 remember—
That time is short, eternity is long.
What good is all the greatness
 of this world at the hour of
 death?
To love You, my God, and
 save my soul is the one thing
 necessary.
Without You, there is no peace,
 no joy.
My God, I need fear nothing
 but sin.
For to lose You, my God, is to
 lose all.
O my God, help me to
 remember—
That to gain all I must leave all,
That in loving You I have all
 good things: the infinite riches
 of Christ and His Church, the
 motherly protection of Mary,
 peace beyond understanding,
 joy unspeakable!

Eternal Father, your Son has
 promised that whatever we ask
 in His Name will be given to
 us. In His Name I pray: give
 me a burning faith, a joyful
 hope, a holy love for Jesus
 Christ. Give me the grace of
 perseverance in doing Your
 will in all things. Do with
 me what You will. I repent of
 having offended You. Grant,
 O Lord, that I may love You
 always and never let me be
 separated from You.
O my God and my All, make me
 a saint!

—A Prayer of
Saint Alphonsus Liguori

Pray It!

Communion of Saints

Many who lose loved ones still feel very close to those who have died. The Church feels the same way. When a Christian is baptized, he or she becomes a member of the Body of Christ. In Baptism a Christian is intimately bound with Jesus and all other Christians. It is a bond that nothing can break—not even death!

This means all the holy ones who have gone before us, and those still alive, join us. When we pray, not only does God hear our prayers, but also many people actually pray for us, multiplying our prayers. This community of prayerfulness is called the Communion of Saints.

Think about the phrases "We're pulling for you," "I'll be thinking of you," "You're in my prayers," and other ways we express our solidarity with, and compassion for, people in our lives. Everyone who has gone before you is pulling for you, all the saints are praying for you, and you are supporting the entire community of faith. Every one of them! Believe it.

Do Not Look to Tomorrow

Do not look forward to what may happen tomorrow. The same Everlasting Father, who takes care of you today, will take care of you tomorrow, and every day. He will either shield you from suffering or give you unfailing strength to bear it. Be at peace, then, and put aside all anxious thoughts and imaginations!

The Everlasting God has in His wisdom foreseen from eternity the cross He now presents to you as a gift from His inmost Heart. This cross He now sends you He has considered with His all-knowing eyes, understood with His divine mind, tested with His wise justice, warmed with loving arms and weighed with His own Hands, to see that it be not one inch too large and not one ounce too heavy for you. He has blessed it with His Holy Name, anointed it with His grace, perfumed it with His consolation, taken one last glance at you and your courage, and then sent it to you from heaven, a special greeting from God to you, an alms of the all-merciful love of God.

—Saint Francis de Sales

Take Me, Give Me

Lord, take me from myself and give me to yourself.

—Saint Catherine of Siena

Take, O Lord, and Receive

Take, O Lord, and receive my entire liberty, my memory, my understanding and my whole will. All that I am and all that I possess You have given me: I surrender it all to You to be disposed of according to Your will. Give me only Your love and Your grace; with these I will be rich enough, and will desire nothing more. Amen.

—Saint Ignatius of Loyola

Grant, O Lord, That My Heart

Grant, O Lord, that my heart may neither desire nor seek anything but what is necessary for the fulfillment of Thy holy Will. May health or sickness, riches or poverty, honors or contempt, humiliations, leave my soul in that state of perfect detachment to which I desire to attain for Thy greater honor and Thy greater glory. Amen.

—Saint Ignatius of Loyola

O My God, Teach Me

O my God, teach me to be
 generous:
to serve you as you deserve
 to be served;
to give without counting
 the cost;
to fight without fear of being
 wounded;
to work without seeking rest;
and to spend myself without
 expecting any reward,
but the knowledge that I am
 doing your holy will.

—Saint Ignatius of Loyola

Fire of God

O ardent fire of my God, which
contains, produces, and imprints
those living ardors which attract
the humid waters of my soul,
and dry up the torrents of earthly
delights, and afterwards soften
my hard self-opinionatedness,
which time has hardened so
exceedingly!

O consuming fire, which even
amid ardent flames imparts
sweetness and peace to the soul!
In you, and in none other, do
we receive this grace of being
reformed to the image and like-
ness in which we were created.

O burning furnace, in which we
enjoy the true vision of peace,
which tries and purifies the gold
of the elect, and leads the soul to
seek eagerly for its highest good,
even thyself, in thy eternal truth.

—Saint Gertrude the Great

Prayer for Peace

O blessed Jesus,
give me stillness of soul in You.
Let your mighty calmness reign
 in me.
Rule me, O You,
 King of Gentleness,
King of Peace.

—Saint John of the Cross

In God's Service

Lord God,
whose we are and whom
 we serve,
help us to glorify you this day,
in all the thoughts of our hearts,
in all the words of our lips,
and in all the works of our hands,
as becomes those who are your
 servants,
through Jesus Christ our Lord.

—Saint Anselm

Relics

After a friend or family member has died, many people continue to visit the grave of that person or cherish one of the person's belongings—a ring, a scarf, a journal. Those visits and possessions keep our memory of that person alive in our hearts. We would certainly not forget a person without those items, but they do help us feel connected to those who have died and can help us embody the qualities we admired.

A relic is an actual item from a saint. This could include an article of clothing, a personal item, or even his or her remains, such as bones. Sometimes relics of a saint are kept in special churches or other places people can visit.

The earliest Christians went to the graves of those who were martyred because of their love for Jesus. It was a way to honor their sacrifice and also a prayer that the living Christians would have the same virtue and love for Jesus that the martyrs possessed.

Study It!

Christ Be within Me

Be within me, every part,
in my mind, my voice, my heart,
in my mouth, on my lips, even in
my fingertips.
Christ be in my eyes, and ears—
to bless my joys,
to calm my fears.
Be with me through this
busy day
in all I think, and do, and say.
It matters not by day or night,
if you are with me, I'll do
all right.
And the world will be a better
place
if you are shining through
my face.

—Saint Jane de Chantal

Prayer On Finding God

Too late have I loved you,
O Beauty so ancient, O Beauty
so new.
Too late have I loved you!
You were within me but I was
outside myself,
and there I sought you!
In my weakness I ran after the
beauty of the things you
have made.

You were with me, and I was not
with you.
The things you have made kept
me from you,
the things which would have
no being unless they existed
in you!
You have called, you have cried,
and you have pierced my deafness.
You have radiated forth, you have
shined out brightly,
and you have dispelled my
blindness.
You have sent forth your fragrance,
and I have breathed it in, and I
long for you.
I have tasted you, and I hunger
and thirst for you. You have
touched me, and I ardently
desire your peace.

—Saint Augustine

Saint Perpetua

About AD 202, the Roman authorities imprisoned Saint Perpetua for being a Christian. When she was arrested, she was preparing to be baptized. Even though not yet baptized, she refused to denounce her faith. She prayerfully considered that she would not survive if she continued to proclaim her belief in Jesus Christ. Her heartbroken father urged her to deny her faith. She simply refused.

Perpetua knew that God would not leave her side. She placed her trust in God and accepted the Romans' punishment for being a Christian. By turning to God wholeheartedly, she was filled with peace and joy even in the midst of torture. God gave her the strength to endure terrible things by helping her to focus on God's love for her.

After having her children taken from her, Perpetua was sent to the wild beasts in front of roaring crowds. She died at the age of twenty-two.

Martyrs like Perpetua believe their faith is worth dying for so we will know that our faith is worth living for!

Live It!

Saint Francis of Assisi

Make Me an Instrument

O Lord, make me an instrument of your peace.
Where there is hatred, let me sow love;
where there is injury, pardon;
where there is doubt, faith;
where there is despair, hope;
where there is darkness, light;
where there is sadness, joy.

O Divine Master, grant that I may not so much seek to be consoled as to console;
to be understood as to understand;
to be loved as to love.

For it is in giving that we receive;
it is in pardoning that we are pardoned;
and it is in dying that we are born to eternal life.
Amen.

—Saint Francis of Assisi

8 Creeds and Devotions

The Apostles' Creed

I believe in God,
the Father almighty,
Creator of heaven and earth,
and in Jesus Christ, his only Son,
 our Lord,
who was conceived by the
 Holy Spirit,
born of the Virgin Mary,
suffered under Pontius Pilate,
was crucified, died and was
 buried;
he descended into hell;
on the third day he rose again
 from the dead;
he ascended into heaven,
and is seated at the right hand of
 God the Father almighty;
from there he will come to judge
 the living and the dead.
I believe in the Holy Spirit,
the holy catholic Church,
the communion of saints,
the forgiveness of sins,
the resurrection of the body,
and life everlasting. Amen.

The Nicene Creed

I believe in one God,
the Father almighty,
maker of heaven and earth,
of all things visible and invisible.

I believe in one Lord Jesus Christ,
the Only Begotten Son of God,
born of the Father before all ages.
God from God, Light from Light,
true God from true God,
begotten, not made,
 consubstantial with the Father;
through him all things were made.
For us men and for our salvation
he came down from heaven,
and by the Holy Spirit was
 incarnate of the Virgin Mary,
and became man.
For our sake he was crucified
 under Pontius Pilate,
he suffered death and was buried,
and rose again on the third day
in accordance with the Scriptures;

He ascended into heaven
and is seated at the right hand
 of the Father.

He will come again in glory
to judge the living and the dead
and his kingdom will have
 no end.

I believe in the Holy Spirit, the
 Lord, the giver of life,
who proceeds from the Father
 and the Son,
who with the Father and the Son
 is adored and glorified,
who has spoken through the
 prophets.

I believe in one, holy, catholic
 and apostolic Church.
I confess one Baptism for the
 forgiveness of sins
and I look forward to the
 resurrection of the dead
and the life of the world to come.
Amen.

Chaplet of the Divine Mercy

*Similar to the Rosary, a chaplet is a
series of repeated prayers in which
a string of beads is used. Early in
the twentieth century, a humble
Polish woman received visions of
Jesus. In those visions, Jesus spoke to
her about his mercy and his desire
to give mercy. The following chaplet
flows from those visions and is given
to advance the three reasons for the*

*visions: to give God's mercy, to urge
us to be merciful, and to urge all
people to trust in Jesus. This prayer
uses rosary beads and begins in the
following manner:*

- *Make the Sign of the Cross.*
- *Pray the Lord's Prayer.*
- *Pray the Hail Mary.*
- *Pray the Apostles' Creed.*

*On the single bead before each
decade, say:*

Eternal Father, I offer You the
 Body and Blood, Soul and
 Divinity of Your dearly
 beloved Son, Our Lord Jesus
 Christ, in atonement for
 our sins and those of the
 whole world.

On the ten beads of each decade, say:

For the sake of His sorrowful
 Passion, have mercy on us and
 on the whole world.

*After praying the five decades, con-
clude by repeating three times:*

Holy God, Holy Mighty One,
 Holy Immortal One, have
 mercy on us and on the
 whole world.
Amen.

Praying with Icons

As beings with five senses, we must use those senses to appreciate things fully. Focusing on icons is an ancient form of prayer that engages our sense of sight. Icons have been part of the Christian tradition for centuries.

An icon is a religious image—usually of Christ but also of Mary—or the saints painted primarily on wood. Icons are not simply religious art; they are a way into contemplative prayer and are therefore one way to let God speak to us. Icons are carefully painted by an iconographer according to exact and ancient rules about color and design. The piece of wood itself is not sacred; rather the one portrayed in the image (who dwells in Heaven) is sacred.

Icons serve as a window into Heaven, connecting us with God, as well as a window from Heaven to earth, allowing us an intimate connection with God.

The way to pray with an icon is by gazing. As we gaze, the icon begins to speak and to reveal its sacred meaning. Praying with icons is another way to present ourselves to Christ or the saints. It is a tool of prayer, helping us to focus on the holy.

© Andrei Rublev Museum, Moscow, Russia / The Bridgeman Art Library

Pray It!

Prayer before a Crucifix

Look down upon me, good and
 gentle Jesus, while before
 Your face I humbly kneel and,
 with burning soul, pray and
 beseech You to fix deep in
 my heart lively sentiments of
 faith, hope, and charity; true
 contrition for my sins; and a
 firm purpose of amendment.

While I contemplate, with great
 love and tender pity, Your
 five most precious wounds,
 ponder over them within me
 and calling to mind the words
 which David, Your prophet,
 said to You, my Jesus:

"They have pierced My hands
 and My feet, they have
 numbered all My bones."

Saint Michael Prayer

Saint Michael the Archangel,
 defend us in battle.
Be our defense against the
 wickedness
 and snares of the devil.
May God rebuke him,
 we humbly pray;
and do thou, O Prince of the
 Heavenly Host,
 by the power of God,
cast into hell, Satan and all the
 evil spirits,
 who roam throughout the
 world
 seeking the ruin of souls.
Amen.

Novenas

Nine days—what good could possibly come from a prayer lasting nine whole days?

Well, lots of good!

A novena is a process of praying for nine consecutive periods of time (typically nine days in a row). This planned time of prayer includes periods of reflection on a specific need or petition.

Novenas are based on the nine days Mary and the disciples waited for the coming of the Holy Spirit after Jesus' Ascension, when he was taken up into Heaven. On that occasion, Jesus had promised his followers that the Holy Spirit would come upon them so that they could witness to him throughout the world. While they waited for the coming of the Spirit, the Apostles and the women followers of Jesus, including his mother, Mary, devoted themselves to prayer.

Have you ever waited so long for something that it seemed like an eternity? What do you do in the passing of time? Do you wish and hope that things were different and worry about what might come, or do you wait patiently, focus on the present, and trust in God's grace, love, and compassion?

Study It!

"Anima Christi"

Soul of Christ, sanctify me.
Body of Christ, save me.
Blood of Christ, inebriate me.
Water from the side of Christ,
 wash me.
Passion of Christ, strengthen me.
Good Jesus, hear me.
Within your wounds hide me.
Never permit me to be separated
 from you.
From the wicked enemy, defend
 me.
At the hour of my death, call me
 and bid me come to you.
That with your Saints I may
 praise you
Forever and ever. Amen.

The Chaplet of Unity

Using the rosary, pray this chaplet in hopes of achieving unity among your family, class, friends, or church group. Split a group of people into two. On each large bead, pray the following:

Group 1: God our Heavenly Father, through your Son Jesus, our Victim—High Priest, True Prophet, and Sovereign King,

Group 2: Pour forth the power of your Holy Spirit upon us and open our hearts. In your Great Mercy,

through the Motherly Mediation of the Blessed Virgin Mary, our Queen, forgive our sinfulness, heal our brokenness, and renew our hearts in the faith, and peace, and love, and joy of your Kingdom, that we may be one in You.

On each of the ten small beads for the five decades, pray the following:

Group 1: In your Great Mercy,

Group 2: Forgive our sinfulness, heal our brokenness, and renew our hearts that we may be one in You.

After the five decades have been prayed, conclude in unison:

Hear, O Israel! The Lord Our
 God is One God!
Oh Jesus, King of All Nations,
 may your reign be recognized
 on Earth!
Mary, Our Mother and Mediatrix
 of All Grace, pray and
 intercede for us your children!
Saint Michael, great prince and
 guardian of your people, come
 with the holy angels and saints
 and protect us!

The Seven Last Words upon the Cross

This devotion can be used individually or with groups to meditate on the meaning of the last words Jesus said while dying on the Cross. It can be prayed anytime during the year but can be especially fruitful during the season of Lent.

V. Come unto my help, O God.

R. O Lord, make haste to help me.

V. Glory to the Father, and to the Son, and to the Holy Spirit,

As it was in the beginning, is now and will be forever.

Amen.

The First Word

"Father, forgive them, they know not what they do." (Luke 23:34)

V. We adore you, O Christ, and we bless you.

R. Because by your holy Cross you have redeemed the world.

Leader: O beloved Jesus, who for the love of me agonized on the cross that you might pay by your sufferings the debt due to my sins, and opened your divine mouth to obtain my pardon from eternal justice: have mercy on all the faithful in their agony, and on me also when I shall be in that extremity, and, through the merits of your most Precious Blood shed for our salvation, give us so lively a sorrow for our sins that we may breathe out our souls into the bosom of your infinite mercy.

Glory be (three times)

V. Have mercy on us, O Lord.

V. Have mercy on us.

All: O my God, I believe in you, I hope in you, I love you, and I repent of having offended you by my sins.

The Second Word

"Amen, I say to you, today you will be with me in Paradise." (Luke 23:43)

V. We adore you, O Christ, and we bless you.

R. Because by your holy Cross you have redeemed the world.

Leader: O beloved Jesus, who for the love of me agonized on the cross, and with readiness and

bounty responded to the faith of the Good Thief, who in the midst of your humiliation acknowledged you to be the Son of God: you who assured him of Paradise, have mercy on all the faithful in their agony, and on me also when I shall be in that extremity, and, through the merits of your most Precious Blood, revive in our souls a faith so firm and constant that it may not waver at any suggestion of the devil, so that we also may obtain the blessed reward of heaven.

Glory be (three times)

V. Have mercy on us, O Lord.

V. Have mercy on us.

All: O my God, I believe in you, I hope in you, I love you, and I repent of having offended you by my sins.

The Third Word

"Woman, behold, your son. . . . Behold, your Mother." (John 19:26–27)

V. We adore you, O Christ, and we bless you.

R. Because by your holy Cross you have redeemed the world.

Leader: O beloved Jesus, who for the love of me agonized on the

cross, and, forgetting your sufferings, left us as a pledge of your love, your own most holy Mother, that through her we might confidently have recourse to you in our greatest need: have mercy on all the faithful in their agony, and on me also when I shall be in that extremity, and, through the interior martyrdom of this, your dear Mother, awaken in our hearts a firm hope in the infinite merits of your most Precious Blood, that we may avoid the eternal damnation which our sins have deserved.

Glory be (three times)

V. Have mercy on us, O Lord.

V. Have mercy on us.

All: O my God, I believe in you, I hope in you, I love you, and I repent of having offended you by my sins.

The Fourth Word

"My God, my God, why have you forsaken me?" (Matthew 27:46)

V. We adore you, O Christ, and we bless you.

R. Because by your holy Cross you have redeemed the world.

Leader: O beloved Jesus, who for the love of me agonized on

the cross, and, heaping suffering on suffering, endured with infinite patience not only your many bodily tortures, but the most heavy affliction of spirit through the forsaking of your Eternal Father: have mercy on all the faithful in their agony, and on me also when I shall be in that extremity, and, through the merits of your most Precious Blood, give us grace to suffer with true patience all the pains and afflictions of our agony, that, uniting them with yours, we may be partakers of your glory in paradise.

Glory be (three times)

V. Have mercy on us, O Lord.

V. Have mercy on us.

All: O my God, I believe in you, I hope in you, I love you, and I repent of having offended you by my sins.

The Fifth Word

"I thirst." (John 19:28)

V. We adore you, O Christ, and we bless you.

R. Because by your holy Cross you have redeemed the world.

Leader: O beloved Jesus, who agonized on the cross for the love

of me, and who, not satisfied with all the ignominy and suffering, willingly would have suffered yet more, so that all might be saved—as was clearly proved when all the torrents of your Passion would not allay the Thirst of your tender Heart: have mercy on all the faithful in their agony, and on me also when I shall be in that extremity, and, through the merits of your most Precious Blood, enkindle such a fire of charity in our hearts as may cause them to burn with the desire of uniting themselves to you for all eternity.

Glory be (three times)

V. Have mercy on us, O Lord.

V. Have mercy on us.

All: O my God, I believe in you, I hope in you, I love you, and I repent of having offended you by my sins.

The Sixth Word

"It is finished." (John 19:30)

V. We adore you, O Christ, and we bless you.

R. Because by your holy Cross you have redeemed the world.

Leader: O beloved Jesus, who for the love of me agonized on

the cross, and from the throne of truth announced the completion of the work of our redemption, through which, from being the children of wrath and perdition, we have become the children of God and the heir of heaven: have mercy on all the faithful in their agony, and on me also when I shall be in that extremity, and through the merits of your most Precious Blood, detach us entirely from the world and from ourselves, and at the moment of our agony give us grace sincerely to offer you the sacrifice of our life in expiation for our sins.

Glory be (three times)

V. Have mercy on us, O Lord.

V. Have mercy on us.

All: O my God, I believe in you, I hope in you, I love you, and I repent of having offended you by my sins.

The Seventh Word

"Father, into your hands I commend my spirit." (Luke 23:46)

V. We adore you, O Christ, and we bless you.

R. Because by your holy Cross you have redeemed the world.

Leader: O beloved Jesus, who agonized on the cross for love of me, and who, in completing this great sacrifice, accepted the will of your Eternal Father, by resigning your spirit into His hands, and then bowing your head and dying: have mercy on all the faithful in their agony, and on me also when I shall be in that extremity, and, through the merits of your most Precious Blood, give us, in our agony, an entire conformity to the divine will, that we may be ready either to live or die according as it will best please you, desiring nothing but the accomplishment of your blessed will in us.

Glory be (three times)

V. Have mercy on us, O Lord.

V. Have mercy on us.

All: O my God, I believe in you, I hope in you, I love you, and I repent of having offended you by my sins.

—FROM *MANUAL OF PRAYERS*, 1996

The Iconographer

"'Theology in imagery,' the icon expresses through color what the Gospel proclaims in words" (Michael Quenot, *The Icon*, p. 12). Because of the seriousness of icons, the rules for creating them are rigorous. The person who paints the holy image, called an iconographer, prepares to paint an icon with a strict discipline of prayer and fasting.

Because the iconographers do not accept personal recognition for the work, they do not sign it. The painting of an icon is not a personal interpretation. Icons are painted using a particular style and process that has survived centuries of tradition. Icons look similar to one another because an iconographer retains and follows this tradition. It has long been believed that Saint Luke painted the first icons of Mary and Jesus and therefore had firsthand knowledge of the shape and look of their faces. All other iconographers add a minimal amount of personal style but mostly use other icons as a guide in painting a new icon.

An iconographer uses the following prayer prior to painting:

O Divine Master of all that exists, enlighten and direct the soul, the heart and the mind of your servant: guide my hands so that I might portray worthily and perfectly your Image, that of your Holy Mother and of all the saints, for the glory, the joy, and the beautification of Your Holy Church. (*The Icon*, p. 13)

Live It!

9 Prayers That Express Our Love for God

Act of Hope

O my God,
trusting in your infinite goodness
 and promises, I hope to
 obtain pardon for my sins, the
 help of your grace, and life
 everlasting, through the merits
 of Jesus Christ, my Lord and
 Redeemer.

Act of Love

O my God,
I love you above all things, with
 my whole heart and soul,
 because you are all-good and
 worthy of all my love. I love
 my neighbor as myself for love
 of you. I forgive all who have
 injured me, and I ask pardon
 for all whom I have injured.
Amen.

Act of Contrition

My God, I am sorry for my sins
with all my heart, and I detest
 them.
In choosing to do wrong and
 failing to do good,
I have sinned against you,
whom I should love above
 all things.
I firmly intend, with your help,
to do penance, to sin no more,
and to avoid whatever leads me
 to sin.
Our savior Jesus Christ suffered
 and died for us.
In his name, my God, have mercy.

Today I Resolve

Lord,
Today I resolve to do the good
You created me to do,
To see the good
You created me to see,
To be the good
You created me to be.
Amen.

The Sacrament of Penance and Reconciliation

Regrettably the Sacrament of Penance and Reconciliation is often misunderstood. This Sacrament of healing, forgiveness, and restoration is about much more than telling the priest our sins. The telling isn't the focus of the Sacrament; rather, the focus is the forgiveness we receive. The nucleus is not our sins, but is God's mercy! It is about the forgiveness God gives and the grace we receive so we can resolve to "sin no more."

Reconciliation heals our relationship with God and keeps our connection with God strong. When we do something wrong, we often become ashamed and embarrassed. We can find it hard to face God.

Jesus made an interesting remark to Peter when predicting Peter's denial. He said, "But I have prayed that your own faith may not fail; and you, and once you have turned back, you must strengthen your brothers" (Luke 22:32). In other words, Jesus recognized that Peter's guilt might have been so overwhelming that he might have begun to think he could not be forgiven and his faith might fail.

The question isn't whether God will forgive us. The question is whether we have the courage to face ourselves honestly, so we can ask for the forgiveness that God is always ready to give. Don't let your faith fail—turn back to Jesus.

Isaiah 1:18: God's Promise

Come now, let us set things right,
 says the LORD:
Though your sins be like scarlet,
 they may become white as snow;
Though they be red like crimson,
 they may become white as wool.

Prayer of Abandonment

Father,
I abandon myself into your hands;
do with me what You will.
Whatever You may do, I thank
 you.

I am ready for all, I accept all.
Let only your will be done in me
and in all your creatures.
I wish no more than this, O Lord.

Into your hands I commend
 my soul;
I offer it to you
with all the love of my heart,
for I love you, Lord,
and so,
I need to give myself,
to surrender myself,
into your hands
without reserve
and with boundless confidence,
for you are my Father.
Amen.

—BLESSED CHARLES

Matthew 5:14–16: Be Light

"You are the light of the world. A
city set on a mountain cannot be
hidden. Nor do they light a lamp
and then put it under a bushel
basket; it is set on a lampstand,
where it gives light to all in the
house. Just so, your light must
shine before others, that they
may see your good deeds and
glorify your heavenly Father."

Act of Faith

O my God,
I firmly believe you are one
 God in three Divine Persons,
 Father, Son, and Holy Spirit.
I believe in Jesus Christ, your
 Son, who became man and
 died for our sins, and who will
 come to judge the living and
 the dead.
I believe these and all the truth
 which the Holy Catholic
 Church teaches, because you
 have revealed them, who
 can neither deceive nor be
 deceived.
Amen.

The Road Ahead

My Lord God,
I have no idea where I am going.
I do not see the road ahead of me.
I cannot know for certain where
 it will end.
Nor do I really know myself,
and the fact that I think I am
following your will
does not mean that I am actually
 doing so.
But I believe that the desire to
 please you
does in fact please you.
And I hope that I have that desire
in all that I am doing.
I hope that I will never do
 anything
apart from this desire.
And I know that if I do this,
you will lead me by the right
 road,
though I may know nothing
 about it.
Therefore I will trust you always,
though I may seem to be lost
and in the shadow of death.
I will not fear,
for you are with me
and you will never leave me to
 face my perils alone.

—Thomas Merton,
Thoughts in Solitude, p. 83

Sacred Heart Prayer

Jesus, meek and humble of heart,
I ask that I may love you more
 and more!
O heart of Jesus, burning with
 love for me,
may my heart burn with love
 for you.
O Sacred Heart of Jesus, may you
 be known
and loved throughout the world!
Amen.

Prayer of Serenity

God, grant me the serenity
to accept the things I cannot
 change,
courage to change the things I can,
and wisdom to know the difference.
Living one day at a time,
enjoying one moment at a time,
accepting hardship as a pathway
 to peace,
taking, as Jesus did,
this sinful world as it is,
not as I would have it,
trusting that You will make all
 things right
if I surrender to your will,
so that I may be reasonably
 happy in this life
and supremely happy in the next.
Amen.

—Reinhold Niebuhr

Preparing to Celebrate the Sacrament of Penance and Reconciliation

The more honest a person is with himself or herself, the more meaningful the person will find the Sacrament of Penance and Reconciliation to be.

When you began to learn about the Sacrament of Penance and Reconciliation, you learned the term *examination of conscience*. Over the years, you may have learned many ways to examine your conscience. Here is a simple reflection that will help you prepare for the Sacrament of Penance and Reconciliation. In the following passage from 1 Corinthians 13:4–7, put your name in place of the words *love* and *it*. Honestly facing yourself with this examination will help you see the areas in your life that have not been transformed into love. Then you will able to experience the healing, forgiveness, and restoration the Lord offers in this sacrament.

> Love is patient; love is kind; love is not envious or boastful or arrogant or rude. It does not insist on its own way; it is not irritable or resentful; it does not rejoice in wrongdoing, but rejoices in the truth. It bears all things, believes all things, hopes all things, endures all things.

Prayer for God's Word
(Psalm 19:8–15)

The law of the LORD is perfect,
 refreshing the soul.
The decree of the LORD is
 trustworthy,
 giving wisdom to the simple.
The precepts of the LORD are
 right,
 rejoicing the heart.
The command of the LORD
 is clear,
 enlightening the eye.
The fear of the LORD is pure,
 enduring forever.
The statutes of the LORD are true,
 all of them just;
More desirable than gold,
 than a hoard of purest gold,
Sweeter also than honey
 or drippings from the comb.
By them your servant is warned;
 obeying them brings much
 reward.

Who can detect trespasses?
 Cleanse me from my
 inadvertent sins.
Also from arrogant ones restrain
 your servant;
 let them never control me.
Then shall I be blameless,
 innocent of grave sin.

Let the words of my mouth be
 acceptable,
 the thoughts of my heart
 before you,
 LORD, my rock and my
 redeemer.

Prayer for Renewal
(Psalm 51:11–17)

Turn away your face from my sins;
 blot out all my iniquities.
A clean heart create for me, God;
 renew within me a steadfast
 spirit.
Do not drive me from before
 your face,
 nor take from me your
 holy spirit.
Restore to me the gladness of
 your salvation;
 uphold me with a willing
 spirit.
I will teach the wicked your ways,
 that sinners may return to you.
Rescue me from violent bloodshed,
 God, my saving God,
 and my tongue will sing
 joyfully of your justice.
Lord, you will open my lips;
 and my mouth will proclaim
 your praise.

Saint John Vianney

Saint John Vianney didn't exactly appear to be a man destined for greatness. He found it difficult to be a good student—his classes were hard for him. Though he was a deeply spiritual man, John was labeled as having meager intelligence. He was supposed to go into the military, but just before his regiment was to leave for battle, he went into a church to pray. When he came out, he found his regiment had left without him. John seemed to be a bit of a goof-up. His parents and teachers often had to help him out of one thing or another.

After his ordination into the priesthood, this seemingly insignificant man became a giant. He was assigned to Ars, a town in a remote region of France. He soon became widely known as a priest dedicated to celebrating God's healing in the Sacrament of Penance and Reconciliation. By the end of his life, more than twenty thousand people were visiting this man annually as he spent sixteen to eighteen hours a day celebrating the Sacrament of Penance and Reconciliation.

John Vianney is called "The Curé of Ars." The word curé is the French term for a parish priest, but its root is the Latin word *curatus*—a word for medical care and healing. Because of his healing touch upon the souls in his care, this gentle giant became a bridge through which people could receive forgiveness and unite more fully with God. Today he is the patron saint of priests—a reminder, perhaps, that no matter what other tasks a priest may have, his most important task is the healing of souls.

Live It!

With gratitude sing songs to God.

Colossians

Jesus Christ Is Lord! (Philippians 2:6–11)

Who, though he was in the form of God,
 did not regard equality with God something to be grasped.
 Rather, he emptied himself,
 taking the form of a slave,
 coming in human likeness;
 and found human in appearance,
 he humbled himself,
 becoming obedient to death,
 even death on a cross.

Because of this, God greatly exalted him
 and bestowed on him the name
 that is above every name,
 that at the name of Jesus
 every knee should bend,
 of those in heaven and on earth and under the earth,
 and every tongue confess that
 Jesus Christ is Lord,
 to the glory of God the Father.

10 Prayers from around the World

Prayers from Africa

The Lord Will Take Care of Me

I have given everything to my Master: He will take care of me . . . The best thing for us is not what we consider best, but what the Lord wants of us!

I received the Sacrament of Baptism with such joy that only angels could describe . . .

O Lord, if I could fly to my people and tell them of your Goodness at the top of my voice: oh, how many souls would be won!

If I were to meet the slave-traders who kidnapped me and even those who tortured me, I would kneel and kiss their hands, for if that did not happen, I would not be a Christian and Religious today . . .

The Lord has loved me so much: we must love everyone . . . we must be compassionate!

I can truly say that it was a miracle I did not die, because the Lord has destined me for greater things . . .

Mary protected me even before I knew her!

When a person loves another dearly, he desires strongly to be close to the other: therefore, why be afraid to die? Death brings us to God!

—SAINT JOSEPHINE BAKHITA OF SUDAN

Living in Solidarity

The word *namaste* (nah-mah-STAY) is an Asian word, a word commonly used in yoga that means "the divine in me recognizes the divine in you." Imagine what it might be like if, every time you encountered a person, you stopped for a moment to realize that you are created in God's image, and the person in front of you also is made in God's image. What would happen if you thought that when someone was mean to you or gossiped about you? What would happen if you thought that when you were tempted to sin against someone or thought dishonorable things about another person?

Simple words say so much! We are called to be in solidarity with others by recognizing the divine in them. As the word *namaste* implies, we also need to recognize and notice the divine in ourselves. When we are in solidarity, we are able to see the world—a situation, a person, or even a problem—through another person's eyes. Standing in solidarity means standing together, side by side, facing forward, with each person having equal power and equal responsibility.

We can live in solidarity with other people when we include them and their needs in our prayer instead of always asking for something we want for ourselves.

Pray It!

Light a Holy Fire

Receive this holy fire.
Make your lives like this fire.
A holy life that is seen.
A life of God that is seen.
A life that had no end.
A life that darkness does
 not overcome.
May this light of God in
 you grow.
Light a fire that is worthy
 of your heads.
Light a fire that is worthy
 of your children.
Light a fire that is worthy
 of your fathers.
Light a fire that is worthy
 of your mothers.
Light a fire that is worthy
 of God.
Now go in peace.
May the Almighty protect you
 today and always.

—DESMOND TUTU, *AN AFRICAN
PRAYER BOOK*, P. 128, FROM
MAASAI, TANZANIA

Father, Thank You

Father, thank you for your
 revelation about death and
 illness and sorrow.
Thank you for speaking so
 plainly to us, for calling us all

friends and hovering over us;
for extending your arms out
to us.
We cannot stand on our own; we
 fall into death without you.
 We fall from faith, left to our
 own. We are really friendless
 without you.
Your extended arms fill us with
 joy, expressing love, love
 caring and carrying, asking
 and receiving our trust.
You have our trust, Father, and
 our faith, with our bodies and
 all that we are and possess.
We fear nothing when with you,
 safe to stretch out and help
 others, those troubled in faith,
 those troubled in body.
Father, help us to do with our
 bodies what we proclaim, that
 our faith be known to you and
 to others, and be effective in
 all the world.

—*AN AFRICAN PRAYER BOOK*,
PP. 65–66, FROM
MAASAI, TANZANIA

Diversity and Unity

Jesus sent a significant and resounding message: love the Lord with all your heart and love your neighbor as you love yourself (see Matthew 22:37–39, Mark 12:29–31, Luke 10:27). During his public ministry, Jesus used stories, parables, and miracles to demonstrate to people that all people, of all races, of all languages are God's beloved people. Jesus revealed that God is Father. With God as our Father, we are brothers and sisters who are united in one family.

Despite this unity, we are also unique. We know that God created us each individually with a mind, heart, and soul. We are each created so uniquely different that no other person will ever be or ever has been just like another. This is amazing to think about, knowing that nearly 6.5 billion people live in the world today. Among these billions of people are diverse cultures with their own dress, dance, food, humor, and prayer.

So which is it, diversity or unity? The answer: Yes!

There is a unity of faith. The Bible says, "There is one body and one Spirit, just as you were called to the one hope of your calling, one Lord, one faith, one baptism, one God and Father of all, who is above all and through all and in all" (Ephesians 4:4–6). Yet this one faith is expressed in a great diversity of ways. From the clarity of thought from Europe to the attention to nature from tribal cultures, from the festive dance of Africa to the elaborate art of Asia, God's people throughout time and the world have brought beautifully rich expression to the human desire to love the Lord with all your heart and love your neighbor as you love yourself.

Study It!

Prayers from Latin and South America

Praise in the Morning

These are the mornings sung
about by David the King!
Today, because it is your saint's
day, we sing to you here.

Wake up, my love, wake up!
Look, the day has already
dawned.
Already the birds are singing.
The moon has already hidden.
How pretty is the morning today
when I come to greet you.

We come all with delight and
pleasure to congratulate you!
The day that you were born all
the flowers were born.
In the baptismal font sang the
nightingales.

The light that God gave is
already dawning.
Get up this morning and look: it
is already dawn!
From all the stars of heaven I
have to bring two:
One to greet you, the other to say
to you goodbye.

Today, because it is your saint's
day, we desire your happiness.
With clusters of flowers I come
to greet you.

And today, because it is your saint's
day, we come to sing to you.

> —*Prayer Without Borders*,
> p. 101, from Mexico

The Wayfarer's Prayer

God, you have guided your people
throughout their history.
So now as pilgrim children we
turn to you, searching for your
image and for a place to rest.
Like a good friend, Lord, you are
always with the poor.
You make yourself a travel
companion to us wayfarers,
to us the undocumented, the
refugees, the migrants, pilgrims
all who walk toward you.
You call us to be witnesses of
your love and to be examples
of our faith in whatever land
receives us.
Lord, may the spirit of Pentecost
be renewed.
May all peoples, races and lan-
guages be one in communion.

> —Youth and Migration
> Program of the Mexican
> Episcopal Commission of
> Youth Ministry, in *Prayer
> Without Borders*, p. 51

Prayer before Sleeping

My guardian angel, my sweet
company, do not abandon me
by night nor by day.

My guardian angel, humbly I
ask you, help me and free me
from all danger.

Four little angels are in my bed, two
at my feet and two at my sides
and the Holy Virgin beside me.

She tells me, "O beautiful child,
sleep and rest, do not be afraid
of anything."

O Blessed Saint Monica, mother of
Saint Augustine, bless my little
bed, because now I go to sleep.

—*Prayer Without Borders*,
p. 49, from Mexico

I Want to Believe, I Will Not Believe

I will not believe in the law of
the strongest, in the language
of guns, in the power of the
powerful.

I want to believe in the rights of
all, in the open hand, in the
strength of the nonviolent.

I will not believe in race or riches,
in privileges, in the established
order.

I want to believe that all human
beings are human beings and
that the order of force and of
injustice is a disorder.

I will not believe that I don't have
to concern myself with what
happens far from here.

I want to believe that the whole
world is my home, the field
that I sow, and that all reap
what all have sown.

I will not believe that I can
combat oppression out there
if I tolerate injustice here.

I want to believe that what is
right is the same here and
there and that I will not be
free while even one human
being is excluded.

I will not believe that war and
hunger are inevitable and that
peace is inaccessible.

I want to believe in the love of
bare hands, in peace on earth.

I will not believe that any effort is
in vain. I will not believe that
the dream of human beings
continues being only a dream
and that death is the end.

But I dare to believe in the dream
of God: a new heaven, a new
earth where justice reigns.

—Dom Helder Camara, in
Prayer Without Borders,
pp. 44–45, from Brazil

Make Me a Better Christian

God the Father, I give you thanks
for all the marvels you have
created.

I praise you and I bless you for
the inestimable grace of life
that you give to us.

Transform me, make me a better
Christian, a living testimony
of your mercy and of your
power.

Strip me, Lord of all roots of
bitterness, of false pride and
haughtiness of heart.

Make me meek and humble of
heart as was our Lord Jesus
Christ, and never let me wound
with my words or my actions
the dignity of any person.

Put in my heart the ardent desire
to work earnestly for the poor
and the needy.

Show me the garment with
which you clothed me the day
that I received you as Lord
and Savior of my life.

May I wear those garments at the
service of my neighbor and of
this community.

Use me, Lord, for your work.

—*Prayer Without Borders*, p. 29,
from El Salvador

Prayer for the Rural and Farming Life

Lord Jesus, in images of farming
and rural life you announced
your gospel to the poor.

We pray for rural men and
women, especially for those
who work hard in the fields.

Give us the strength of your
Spirit to be witnesses and
collaborators of the creative
providence.

May we always sow in ourselves
and in our families the
holiness and hope of Christian
life, with the same zeal with
which we cultivate our land.

Bless the daily efforts of farmers
and farm workers.

Let all recognize the dignity of
their labor.

Raise from among us men and
women at the service of the
gospel, sisters and brothers to
announce unceasingly your
love for this world that is your
own field and farm.

We give you glory forever
and ever.

—*Prayer Without Borders*,
p. 31, from Colombia

Prayers from Europe

An Irish Blessing

May the road rise up to meet
 you,
May the wind be always at
 your back,
May the sun shine warm upon
 your face,

And the rains fall soft upon
 your fields,
And until we meet again,
May God hold you in the palm
 of His hand.

Saint Patrick

Which Way, Lord? What Can I Do?

Patty and Rod were both college-educated adults who had a great deal of concern for others, especially the poor. They felt a desire in their heart to work for justice. Yet despite all their work for the needy, they felt God was calling them to do more. Because of this sense, they simply asked and found their answer. Against the recommendations and fears of their families, they moved to a poor neighborhood.

To identify *more fully* with the poor, they moved into this neighborhood to live side by side *with* the people there, to be with them and to be one with them. Living in such solidarity allowed Patty and Rod to live closest to what Jesus asks of us—to treat everyone with respect and to love one another.

Thirty-five years later, Patty and Rod are still in the same neighborhood and still work together with their neighbors to develop ways to improve their lives through education, justice awareness, spiritual reflection, and, above all, *recognition of* the dignity and value of every human being.

Interestingly, not only have the people of the neighborhood met Jesus in the faces of Patty and Rod, but Patty and Rod have met Jesus in the faces of their neighbors.

Live It!

Prayers from Asia

We Pray This Day

Oh God, we pray this day:
for all who have a song they
cannot sing,
for all who have a burden they
cannot bear,
for all who live in chains they
cannot break,
for all who wander homeless and
cannot return,
for those who are sick and for
those who tend them,
for those who wait for loved ones
and wait in vain,
for those who live in hunger
and for those who will not share
their bread,
for those who are misunderstood
and for those who misunderstand,
for those who are captives and for
those who are captors,
for those whose words of love are
locked within their hearts
and for those who yearn to hear
those words.

Have mercy upon these, O God.
Have mercy upon us all.

—*Kneeling in Jerusalem*,
p. 40, Israel

Prayer to Respect Others

As I walk down dusty roads or
busy concrete boulevards, help
me, God, to take the time to
see in the eyes of the other, to
recognize the other, in order
to respect.
As I encounter many people,
many races, help me to
appreciate the hand of the
other, to recognize those
hands that create and build, in
order to work together.
As my path calls me to various
places, help me to learn to
walk together with others
on paths that lead to peace,
recognizing that by walking
with others, in working
together, we learn to recognize
ourself in the other, to
recognize and appreciate our
differences.
And begin to recognize what love
is about.

—*Prayer Without Borders*,
p. 47, from Pakistan

We Take Time

Oh God, we take time to pause
from daily work to gather
our thoughts; to let our souls
catch up with our bodies;
to feel your presence in our
creation; to ask forgiveness for
our lapses, ours and on behalf
of your people; and to be
ourselves restored.

Breathing in, God's Spirit calms
my body; breathing out, it's
good to be alive.

Lord Jesus Christ, we take time
to gather around you. By your
life and teachings may we find
our strength, and journeying
together may we find our rest.

Breathing in, Christ lives in our
lives; breathing out, it's good
to be alive.

Holy Spirit, creative energy of
love and compassion, life
embracing, life transforming,
heal our bodies, heal our
souls, heal our relationships,
heal our nations.

Breathing in, the Spirit heals;
breathing out, it's good to
be alive.

Amen.

—*Prayer Without Borders*,
p. 93, from the Christian
Conference of Asia

Part III

**METHODS FOR
PERSONAL PRAYER**

11 Praying the Lord's Prayer

The Lord's Prayer

Our Father, who art in Heaven,
hallowed be thy name;
thy kingdom come,
thy will be done
on earth as it is in Heaven.
Give us this day our daily bread,
and forgive us our trespasses,
as we forgive those who trespass
 against us;
and lead us not into temptation,
but deliver us from evil. Amen.

Praying as a Poem

The following is a poetic break-down of the Lord's Prayer. Several synonyms complement each line. Each synonym portrays or points to a further or deeper meaning of the words of the Lord's Prayer. Make this poem a prayer. Pray it slowly and allow each new word to transform your heart. This poem can bring new life to these familiar words, and the "Lord's Prayer" can have a renewed meaning for you. Add any words that are important to you. This poetic interpretation demonstrates that personal prayer is deep, complex, and substantial— even in the simple words of the Lord's Prayer.

Our: community, together, everyone's, group's, family's, us, we, collectively, jointly, equal, mutual

Father: Creator, origin, destina-tion, mother, parent, maker, Abba, God

who art: exists, lives, breathes, moves, stays, is

in Heaven: above, around, in, under, over, everywhere

hallowed be thy name: holy, blessed, special, deep, mean-ingful, sacred, divine, graceful

thy kingdom come: world, ideal, universe, dream, creation, place, space, home, reign

thy will be done: motivation, strength, desire, hope, reason, trust, witness

on earth: here, with, around, above, below, next to, within, nature

as it is in Heaven: the universe, eternity, soul, forever, beyond, over, within

Give us this day: present, now, today, patience, here and now, nearby, current, this moment, for now

our daily bread: nourishment, sustenance, fuel, essentials, needs, necessities

and forgive us our trespasses: sins, dishonor, disrespect, steal dignity

as we forgive those: let go, release, heal, reconcile, renew, try again, purify

who trespass against us: hurt, pain, dishonor, mistrust, abandon, abuse, mislead, discredit, blame, harm

And lead us: guide, teach, show, allow, gentle, point, coach, demonstrate, aim, direct, train

not into temptation: lure, destruction, bitterness, revenge, injustice

but deliver us: free, arrive, carry, send, bring, bear, hold, grasp, endure, support, keep, prevent, protect, rescue

from evil: wrong, sin, wickedness, immorality, unrest, trouble, corruption, offense, attack, malice, hatred

Amen: So be it! Absolutely! You bet! Yes! I believe it! Absolutely! Definitely! I agree!

Matthew 6:9–13

"This is how you are to pray:

Our Father in heaven,
 hallowed be your name,
your kingdom come,
your will be done,
 on earth as in heaven.
Give us today our daily bread;
and forgive us our debts,
 as we forgive our debtors;
and do not subject us to the
 final test,
 but deliver us from the evil one."

Spontaneous Prayer

A large part of prayer is conversation with God. In prayer, we might ask for something or express gratitude. We might simply tell God how great we believe he is, or we might tell God a problem we are having and simply surrender our problems to his wisdom.

When we just don't have the words, we can rely on what we already know. Prayers like the Lord's Prayer and Hail Mary can call us to prayer even when we don't know what to say. But we can also speak with God from our hearts, and we can voice our thoughts just as we would to a friend. Such conversation is called spontaneous prayer.

Spontaneous prayer is a great way to talk with God about anything at all. Don't worry about getting caught up in the words to say. Know that God already knows what you need before you ask (see Matthew 6:8). Know that Jesus found himself in times of deep prayer. Many people feel they can't pray. But if we say "God help me. I'm not good at prayer," we have taken the first step to spontaneous prayer! Pray before school. Pray before tests. Pray with a friend in need. Just be in touch with the present moment and invite God to be a part of it. By doing this, you fulfill Saint Paul's command to pray at all times (see 1 Thessalonians 5:17).

Pray It!

The Lord's Prayer and the Early Church

Jesus gave the Apostles direct information about how to pray effectively. Jesus gave them (and us) the words of the Lord's Prayer, or the Our Father.

The Lord's Prayer is considered the perfect prayer because it encompasses all we are called to as Christians. It is the perfect prayer of asking, because it voices our needs, yet acknowledges that we need God's will to be done most of all.

As the early disciples searched for a way to continue the mission that Jesus began, little did they know they would rely on Jesus' prayer instruction after he had left them and returned to Heaven.

Pray the Lord's Prayer. Think about how this prayer has helped you in the past. If you cannot think of a time, try to identify how the Lord's Prayer might carry you in the future. Commit yourself to praying the perfect prayer every day.

Study It!

A Format for Personal Prayer

As you begin to develop your habits of prayer, trying different styles and structures of prayer can be very exciting. The Lord's Prayer contains seven distinct steps that can be a structure to a daily prayer time.

1. **Our Father in Heaven, hallowed be your name.** Often we pray to God because we are in need of his help. God is the awesome Creator of all, the giver of life and love. Spend this first part of your prayer praising God and thanking God because God is worthy of all praise and worship.

2. **Your kingdom come.** When Jesus preached, he preached Good News. The Good News is that the Reign of God is here and it is among us. We believe this by faith. Our experience, however, tells us that God's Reign hasn't completely come. Spend this part of your prayer asking for God's justice to come. Where are wars? In your community, where are conflicts? How is life, from conception to natural death, threatened? These are some of the things that need prayer.

3. **Your will be done, on earth as it is in Heaven.** Before you were born, God knew you. In fact, God knows you better than anyone. God has a vision of the person you can be and of a life of joy and fullness. But rather than seeking the life God has for them, many people resist. During this time of prayer, ask for God's will to be done in you, a will for happiness, joy, and hope.

4. **Give us this day our daily bread.** Because God loves you more than you can imagine, God wants you to bring your needs to him. Are you having trouble with friends? Do you feel the stress of school or family life? Come to the Lord and speak all of your needs. Just by telling God these things, you are making a great act of faith.

5. **And forgive us our debts, as we also have forgiven our debtors.** Scripture is clear that we can receive forgiveness to the extent that we forgive others. Whom are you mad at? Who has embarrassed you in front of others? Who has betrayed you? The Lord asks you to

Philippians

forgive these people and then to know the fullness of God's forgiveness.

6. **And do not bring us to the time of trial.** Temptation is everywhere we turn—to cheat in school, to lie to our parents, to do things that are against God's will as shown in Scripture and in the Church's teaching. We believe, however, that where temptation is, God's help is there even more. Pray for the help you will need when faced with temptations.

7. **But rescue us from the evil one.** The last petition of the Lord's Prayer continues the theme of the struggle between good and evil. It moves from our personal struggle with evil to pray with the whole Church about the distress of the world. Even when we pray in private, we pray in communion with the whole Church for the needs of the whole human family.

Saint Teresa of Ávila

Saint Teresa of Ávila was a mystic, a teacher of the art of prayer, a spirit-filled leader of a religious order, a woman of great courage, and an individual who lived life to the fullest. Before that, she lost interest in God when she was twelve years old. At age fifteen, her mother died, and Teresa was placed in the care of Augustinian nuns. With these women, her love of God was rekindled.

Throughout her life, Teresa struggled with repeated illnesses, and she struggled with prayer. But in her forties, she was deeply transformed by prayer, in fact, by the Lord's Prayer.

Sometimes the Lord's Prayer can become such a routine prayer that we don't even listen to the words we are saying. But Teresa found that by joining these words to a mind focused on God, a person could know an intimate, mystical friendship with God. Teresa spoke of prayer as an intimate sharing between friends. Prayer is taking time frequently to be alone with God and having the Lord's Prayer as the basis of the conversation between friends.

Live It!

12 Praying with Scripture: Lectio Divina

Some people think of the Bible as written in stone, like the stone tablet with the Ten Commandments that Moses carried down the mountain. There is a comfort in thinking of things that don't change. When you pick up your Bible and read it, you are reading ancient words. In the Old Testament, you have the words that God's people, Israel, read. In the entirety of Scripture, you hold the same words your parents read, the saints have read, and countless men and women throughout the ages have read. When you turn to the Psalms, you are reading the words Jesus read in his prayer time. In many ways, the thought of the Bible as words written in stone is an accurate one, but not completely accurate.

The words of the Bible also are like a river. A river flows through the land and changes everything around it. If you have ever flown over Las Vegas, you know what water does to a desert. You are flying over brown land . . . brown . . . brown . . . suddenly *green!* The water has changed the desert, making it livable and beautiful.

The Word of God flows through your heart, and its ancient truths are meant to change you and the things around you. *Lectio divina*, or "holy reading," is a way of praying with Scripture that allows the words you read to flow into every part of you: thoughts, words, and action; body, mind, and soul.

For many of us, reading is a quick process. We usually try to read fast to cover as much as we can in as short a time as possible. But *lectio divina* is slow. It is a relaxed, deliberate reading that is more about depth than breadth.

Lectio divina begins with developing the ability to listen deeply

and to hear with the ear of your heart. *Lectio divina* requires patience with yourself as you learn to slow down. You learn to quiet down. You learn the rhythm of this form of prayer. *Lectio divina* requires courage, because silence can feel uncomfortable. We live in a noisy world. We get in our cars and turn on the radio. We walk in our homes and turn on the television. The silence of *lectio divina* invites us to push past the discomfort of psychological silence and find the refreshment of spiritual silence.

The question in your heart during *lectio divina* is not "Is God speaking to me?" but rather "What is God saying to me?" In *lectio divina*, you move into the recesses of your heart where God dwells.

The Four R's of Lectio Divina

Introduction

As you begin learning *lectio divina*, you may find it helpful to use the Psalms for your reading. Perhaps you start at the beginning and read a new section each day. Perhaps you use the Psalms for the Mass readings of the day. Remember, *lectio divina* is about depth, not breadth. The passage you choose ought not be too long. Although the form of *lectio divina* is not rigid or set in stone, it does have a four-part process, the four R's: reading (*lectio*), reflecting (*meditatio*), responding (*oratio*), and resting (*contemplatio*).

Reading (*Lectio*)

Begin reading with your heart and mind focused on the God who dwells in the very Word you read. Draw near to the Word with the same reverence with which you approach the Blessed Sacrament at church. With this reverence, read.

And read again . . . and read again . . . and again. You are listening for words or phrases that resonate within your heart. Read your words and phrases aloud. Read what attracts your heart.

Pray It!

Sharper Than Any Two-Edged Sword: Scripture and the Heart

In the movie *The Flintstones* (1994, 91 minutes, rated PG), Fred, Wilma, Barney, and Betty decide to take a trip to the Grand Canyon. They arrive, and there flowing through the rock is a tiny stream, about 2 inches wide, with a sign posted next to it that says "Grand Canyon." "Yeah," says Barney. "They say this will really be something someday."

If you have ever been to the Grand Canyon, you know that Barney was right. The mighty Colorado River has cut into the rock of that canyon, revealing the beauty in its depths.

If you let it, God's Word flowing through your life will change you. It will cut through the things in your life that keep you from being who God has made you to be. Sometimes those things the river needs to cut through are sin and wrongdoing. Other times it has to cut through the limits you put on yourself. Have you ever said to yourself, "I could never . . ." Well, maybe you could. If you let God's Word cut through, it will show you that your heart is as amazing as the Grand Canyon, as powerful, as beautiful.

Reflecting (*Meditatio*)

In reflecting, ponder the words you have read. Imitate Mary, who "kept all these things, reflecting on them in her heart" (Luke 2:19). God's Word is alive with power and meaning. In this step of *lectio divina*, ask yourself, "What does this mean?" or "What does this mean to me?" Let the life of the Word give you life as you consider how the ancient words you read speak to you today.

The temptation of the reflecting step of *lectio divina* is to make it an intellectual exercise. Remember, the primary activity of reflecting is listening. In reflecting, look for God's light shining on the words before you. In this holy light, see in new ways, hear with new ears. In reflecting, "let the word of Christ dwell in you richly" (Colossians 3:16).

Responding (*Oratio*)

You might think of prayer as conversation with God. In the first step, reading, God has spoken to you. In the second step, reflecting, you spend time understanding God's message. In responding, it is your turn. Let your heart speak to God. As you understand the passage, what does it make you want to pray for? Do you want to thank God, praise God, ask God's forgiveness, complain to God, ask for God's help, or pray for others?

Prayer is the cry of your heart. Prayer is tears. Prayer is joy. Prayer is asking. Prayer is offering. Prayer is the gift you give to God.

The Bible as God's Word

You are sitting in Mass, listening to the first reading, the responsorial psalm, the second reading, then, with an "Alleluia!" the congregation stands to greet the Gospel.

Reading the Bible as God's Word means that even if you are sitting on your bed or in your favorite chair, your heart is standing, attentive, because God's Word is different from all other words. God's Word is alive, and it gives life to everything around it—including you.

When we go to Mass, we believe Jesus is truly present in the Eucharist. He also is present in the priest and in the praying and singing of the people. He is also present in the Word. Of these four ways that Jesus is present at Mass, Scripture is the only one you can have with you in your room. Do you want Jesus to be present? Read the Word.

God is speaking to you as you read the Word. What is God saying? Let your heart be standing and attentive.

Study It!

Resting (*Contemplatio*)

Too many times, we are tempted to end our prayer after we have talked, but there is yet another step: resting in the presence of God.

Have you ever been on a long drive with a friend in which the two of you said little? Consider such silence between two friends—the comfort, the solace, the joy of knowing that you are understood, that you are loved. In resting, you realize you have connected with the Spirit of God, and you wait there, you let your heart dwell there, you stay and let God love you.

Perhaps you are concerned: "Will I be able to hear God?" Yes. Remember, your heart was made to find its way to God. "In the same way, the Spirit too comes to the aid of our weakness; for we do not know how to pray as we ought, but the Spirit itself intercedes with inexpressible groanings" (Romans

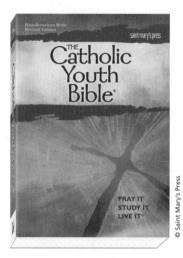
© Saint Mary's Press

8:26). The Spirit prays for us when we have no words of our own and listens for us when we find it hard to hear the words of God. Yes, your heart will find its way to God.

In *lectio divina*, our souls absorb the Word of God. Then it flows from us into the world, giving life and changing everything around us.

The Four R's of *Lectio Divina*

1. Reading (*Lectio*)

Take your time and read the passage. Get a sense of what it is saying. Read the passage a second time. Pause on any words or phrases that strike you, and listen in your heart.

2. Reflecting (*Meditatio*)

As you pause on the words or phrases that strike you, ask yourself the following questions:

- What does this passage mean?
- What does this passage mean to me or for my situation?

3. Responding (*Oratio*)

As you get a sense of the passage's meaning, ask yourself the following questions:

- What does this passage want me to pray for?
- What does this passage make me want to say to God?

4. Resting (*Contemplatio*)

Take time to be attentive to your heart, where God moves, lives, and speaks within you. Ask yourself the following question:

- What do I feel God is saying back to me now that I have responded to God?

Saint Jerome

The next time you pick up your Bible, think of Saint Jerome. He was a priest and scholar who lived in the fourth century AD.

The Pope commissioned Jerome to revise the translation of the Bible. As Catholics, we have had a glimpse of some of the struggles Jerome faced when he revised the Bible, because in recent years the translation we use at Mass has also gone through revisions. Some people do not think the changes are good; others welcome them, believing that the changes make the words more meaningful, perhaps more accurate to their original version.

Jerome had both fans and critics, and the discussions weren't always pleasant. But this scholar loved the Word of God and wanted to make it understood. While some focused on an exact, word-for-word translation of the Bible, Jerome focused on translating the overall meaning.

Jerome raised a great question: "How do you and I make the Word of God understood by the people we meet each day?" As people who believe in God's Word, we are asked to live God's Word in a way that makes God known to those we meet.

Live It!

13 Praying with Guided Meditation

Every moment is alive with God. Every moment, past, present, and future, is full of God's presence and power. Learning to be fully alive to the moment today means you are prepared for the tomorrows to come.

Guided meditation is a prayer form that relies heavily on the imagination. It is also a form of prayer that relies heavily on the senses. Guided meditation awakens you to your surroundings, relationships, feelings, and thoughts. It guides you in prayer to an encounter or an exchange with Jesus, and it helps you become more aware of God's presence in the world after prayer.

Scriptural Meditation

In a guided meditation with a Bible passage, Scripture becomes alive to you. You place yourself into the scriptural account and become a character in the story: a disciple, a bystander, one being healed, or even Jesus.

Getting Started

To begin guided scriptural meditation, choose a Scripture passage. The following may provide some good places to look:

- the Gospel for the day's Eucharistic liturgy (The daily readings from the liturgy can be found at the Web site for the United States Conference of Catholic Bishops.)

- the reading from the upcoming Sunday's Eucharistic liturgy

- a Bible passage someone has given you that means a lot to you

© Saint Mary's Press / Vicki Shuck, illustrator

Genesis

- a passage that was used on a retreat or other event you attended

Once you have selected the passage, take a few moments to call to mind that you are in the presence of God. Turn off radios, phones, and computers, and just sit comfortably.

Imagine that the air you breathe is the Holy Spirit. As you breathe in, you breathe in the Holy Spirit. As you breathe out, you release the noise in your mind or soul.

Continue until you experience calm and peace.

Entering into the Reading

Pick up your Bible and read the passage. Read it more than once, but during this first reading, simply become familiar with the passage.

Read the passage again. This time choose a person in the passage and imagine you are experiencing the story as that person—a disciple, a bystander, someone Jesus is interacting with, or Jesus himself. Use your imaginary senses to pay close attention to the surroundings. Ask yourself the following questions:

- What do I see?
- What do I feel?
- What do I smell?
- What do I hear?
- If the story involves food and drink, what do I taste?

Reacting to the Story

Read the passage again. Pay close attention to your feelings and to the reaction of others in the story.

- How do others react to the situation?
- What do I feel through the action in the story?

- What are my thoughts as this action takes place?

Praying through the Story

Now that you have fully entered into the story with your senses, mind, and feelings, it is time to interact with Jesus beyond the bounds of the story. As you are aware of yourself as a character, what do you want to pray for here and now? Do want to be a better disciple? Do you need to experience Jesus's forgiveness for something you have done? Are you brokenhearted and in need of Jesus' healing? Do you need to heal others as Jesus did? Take time to voice your thoughts and feelings to Jesus and allow him to change you.

Can We Hear God's Voice in Prayer?

Yes, we can hear God's voice in prayer! But are we listening?

God's manner of speaking to his people is as unique as the people themselves. Each of us hears God in our own way, because God speaks to us in a way that we can hear him.

We hear most voices with our ears. God speaks to us through our hearts, through our eyes, and in our souls. God's voice is an impression, a knowing that calls us toward something.

A common obstacle to hearing God is simply this: we often dismiss the ways in which God speaks. A thought goes through our mind that we dismiss as silly. A comment someone makes hits us for a moment, but instead of pausing to reflect or write it down, we go about our day. We see a connection between a Scripture passage we are reading and a situation a friend is facing, but we don't tell the friend because we are afraid the friend will think it is dumb. Listen and act!

Pray It!

Imaginative Prayer through an Event

Scripture offers a ready-made place for you to enter into a story of Jesus. Other events can offer this as well, especially the Sacraments. Although you may not have a memory of your Baptism, you can experience it through your imagination. Ideally, another person would read the following meditation as your imagination guides you through the events. You could certainly lead others through the meditation if you are asked to lead prayer at your church, school, or elsewhere.

This meditation on Baptism can also be used when you are alone. Read it slowly, pray through the following event, and allow yourself to be guided—by Jesus. As it feels natural to you, stop and paint the scene with your mind's eye. Pay attention to your feelings and speak to Jesus from your heart.

Meditation on Your Baptism

You are sitting barefoot at the grassy edge of a river. The weather is beautiful, and it is very peaceful here. You close your eyes, and you feel the heat of the sun on your face. You hear the splashing of the current as the water quickly moves downstream.

A noise close by startles you. You sit up and see a quiet, patient-looking man standing not too far from you. You recognize the beard and eyes, and you realize the man is Jesus. He smiles as he approaches and sits down next to you. He greets you by name. Hear yourself respond to him. Notice how you feel to be with Jesus. Hear him tell you that he is happy to have this time alone with you and that there are things he wants to discuss with you. You watch Jesus as he turns his eyes to look at the river. He tells you the water reminds him of his cousin John, who baptized him in the Jordan River. There is affection on his face and in his voice as he speaks of John.

Listen as Jesus talks with you about his Baptism and where it took him. Hear Jesus share with you some of the highlights of his life.

Now Jesus looks into your eyes. Hear him ask you to renew

Distractions in Prayer

"My mind wanders!" "What's wrong with me? Why can't I stay focused in prayer?" These are often-heard comments when it comes to prayer. We view these mental wanderings as evidence that we are failing at prayer.

What if these mental wanderings are not an obstacle to prayer but, in fact, can be a guide to prayer?

If you are praying and you find your mind has wandered, pause and note what has come to your mind. Perhaps your mind has turned to a particular decision you need to make. Maybe a friend you are worried about comes to mind.

Instead of dismissing the situation, look for a connection between the Scripture passage and the "distraction." For example, if you find yourself thinking about a friend whom you are worried about, there may be something in that Scripture passage that will help your friend.

You can connect the place to which your mind has wandered to the place where you started—namely, your prayer.

Study It!

your baptismal commitment. Trust him as he reminds you that he will be there to help you always. Together you discuss what truly living out your Baptism means. You talk about what areas in your life need changing or improving. Perhaps you talk about relationships . . . or things you've done that you are not proud of . . . or things you haven't done that you could do. . . . Just share with Jesus everything that keeps you from really living your life as a committed Christian.

Jesus now asks you what good things you have done lately and asks you to share the times when you have really followed him.

Listen as Jesus thanks you for your goodness. Hear him tell you how much good you can accomplish in his name. Notice your feelings as Jesus tells you this.

Jesus stands up and bends forward to offer you a hand. He pulls you up to stand beside him. Notice your reaction when Jesus invites you into the water to be renewed. Follow Jesus. As you come closer to the river, you begin to feel the rocky sand under your feet. You smile at each other as you feel the first sensation of

the cold water swirling around your lower legs. You wade in as far as your knees and stop. Cupping both of his palms together, Jesus bends and dips his hands into the water. His eyes sparkle as he pours the cool water over your head. He prays for you. Listen as he prays.

There is a stillness once Jesus has finished his prayer. Jesus does not move but, instead, seems to be waiting for something. His head remains bowed. Then a powerful but gentle voice fills the air. The voice speaks directly to you and seems to surround you on all sides as it proclaims, "This is my beloved child in whom I am well pleased." Allow yourself to remain quiet and take this in. Know that it has been said to you, about you.

—ADAPTED FROM JANE E. ARSENAULT AND JEAN R. CEDOR, LEADER'S GUIDE FOR *GUIDED MEDITATIONS FOR YOUTH ON SACRAMENTAL LIFE*, PP. 11–17

Fr. Walter Burghardt

Hundreds of years from now, Catholics may look at today's time period in the Church and regard Fr. Walter Burghardt as a priest who helped a generation of Catholics learn how to live the Gospel of Jesus Christ.

Burghardt is one of today's most influential preachers. He has urged his listeners to use their belief to make a difference in how they live and in how they relate to the world around them, particularly to those who are less fortunate.

In his writings and homilies, Burghardt enters Scripture through guided meditation and experiences it as fully alive. He looks at not only the main character of the story but also the people and the culture around the story. He then draws on his experience and turns his attention toward today's questions.

Through his fully alive reflection on Scripture, Burghardt invites us to consider what these stories mean for us as individuals and for the Church today.

Live It!

Reflecting on the Meditation

Take some time to reflect on the following questions for the experience to become a part of you:

- How did I feel when Jesus asked me to renew my baptismal commitment?

- What areas of my life did I share with Jesus that need changing or improving if I am to live as a committed Christian?

- When have I faithfully followed Jesus? What good things have I done? What did Jesus say to me after I had shared the good things I have done?

- What were my feelings as Jesus pulled me up and led me into the river?

- What did Jesus say in his prayer for me as he poured the water over my head?

- How did I feel when I heard the voice proclaim, "This is my beloved child in whom I am well pleased"?

14 Prayer and Journaling

Journaling is a spiritual practice that is both self-revealing and God-revealing.

For those who are committed to growing in prayer, in relationship with God, and in understanding of how God works in their life, journaling can be a critical piece. Once pen touches paper, it is amazing what things flow out.

In addition to building your spiritual life, journaling helps empty you of the present day and start tomorrow with a clean slate. In your journal, you can pour your heart out to God, who always hears and receives you.

A journal can help you stay thankful to God. Isn't it easy to forget about the prayers God has answered? By writing your prayers in your journal—both petitions and thanks—you remain ever grateful to God, because your journal reminds you of what God has done.

Journaling takes a bit of practice to do well. Certainly, those who are writers by nature adopt the practice more quickly, but anyone can learn to journal in a way that is both helpful and meaningful. To develop any good habit, you must do the same thing repeatedly until you do it instinctively. For example, let's say that for the last month, you have taken 5 minutes to journal before going to bed. One night you are in bed and you feel as though you have forgotten something. Your journal! You know you have a good habit if you miss it when it is gone.

Pray It!

Personal Salvation History

In the Old Testament Book of Deuteronomy, you often see the word *remember*. The Hebrew people living in the Promised Land were urged to continually remember the good things God had done for them.

In the same way, you need to look at the past to see how God guided and still guides your personal history. This history is the story of your life in God, your salvation!

One method for exploring your salvation history is to brainstorm a list of the most important events of your life—from your earliest memories to your most recent significant moments. What is an important event? You be the judge. It might be an accident, an award, a meeting with a friend, a crisis in your family, an accomplishment, a revealing conversation. Be as thorough as possible in making your list.

In your desire to be closer to God, it can be tempting to think you need a "religious experience" to know God's love for you. These experiences happen for some on retreats or at the Eucharist. For many, such overwhelming experiences do not happen. Rather, God's love is seen over time. After finishing your list, read it over slowly. How has God shown love for you over time? This is your personal salvation history. (Adapted from Carl Koch, *PrayerWays*, p. 94)

Getting Started

Decide on a Journal

As you begin your practice of journaling, choose a journal that is comfortable for you to write in. For example, people often prefer a spiral binding with a hard back. You will also want to decide where you will keep your journal. It is important to treat your journal respectfully; it will carry things from the deepest part of you.

Choose the Right Time of Day

The next step is deciding when you will journal. This takes a bit of practice to see what works best for you. Some prefer the morning, when they can pour out their hopes for the day. Others prefer the evening, when journaling becomes an examining and emptying exercise. Perhaps you will find that a bit of both works for you.

How you use your journaling time also requires some work to see what works best for you. If journaling is new for you, you may find one of the following formats a helpful way to begin.

Journaling in the Morning

At the conclusion of your morning prayer, take a moment and write in your journal the impressions you had from your prayer, ways you felt God might be speaking, or things you think God may be asking you to do. Finally, write a prayer of offering, giving God your heart and your day.

Journaling in the Evening

Write a list of those things you remember from your day, the moments that seemed significant, even if you don't know why. If you recorded a morning journal entry, read your entry to see if those moments from your day connect with anything from your morning prayer. Write about the connections you see. Finally, write a prayer to God, letting go of your day by placing it in God's hands. Ask God to use your sleep to heal you and draw you closer to God.

Feelings in Prayer

The feelings you experience during prayer can be an entryway into deeper prayer. Think of it this way: when something happens, your first reaction isn't verbal; rather, it is in your gut—your feelings.

How do you think you would feel if you found out a friend talked about you behind your back? You might *feel* the hurt before you *talked about* the hurt. What do your feelings reveal about you? They reveal that you love your friend. They show that you know betrayal is not part of a good friendship.

Prayer requires everything of you: thoughts, body, soul, and feelings. Your feelings in prayer can help you realize things that are not at the surface.

Some people are surprised to experience loneliness during prayer. Isn't this the opposite of the feeling you should have? Why is loneliness present? If you examine yourself, you might find that the loneliness reveals that you have an ability to follow God even when it is difficult.

What feelings do you have in prayer? What do they reveal about you and what you believe? Take a moment with your journal and reflect on your feelings. You might understand yourself and God in a deeper way.

Study It!

Try Different Techniques

You can use several techniques in journaling. Similar to finding the right time to write, finding the technique that works best for you and your style is helpful. Look over these different styles and experiment with them. You may find that a particular style works well, but not all the time. Refer to these styles often. You may find that the technique depends on your mood.

Free Writing

Free writing means exactly that— writing freely and spontaneously whatever comes to mind, letting ideas and feelings flow out unchecked. When free writing, try to write continuously, hardly lifting pen from paper. If you get stuck, write a word or phrase over and over until something else comes to mind.

Try to take a playful attitude toward this sort of journal writing. Chances are, you will uncover some surprises, and that is the point of free writing. After free writing, you may decide to examine one of the surprises further, using another journal-writing technique.

Composing Unsent Letters

If you have ever been furious with someone but knew you could not tell the person of your anger directly, or if you have ever fallen madly in love but were afraid to

© Nekrasow Andrey / shutterstock.com

express your feelings out loud, then you probably can understand the value of writing a letter that will not be sent. Sometimes just the exercise of writing can help get rid of your anger or name your love.

Writing unsent letters in your journal gives you a chance to say anything to anyone, especially to God. Also, writing unsent letters gives you a sense of having an audience with whom to communicate. Many of us find writing to a person easier than just writing on a blank sheet of paper.

Writing Dialogue

Even when you do free writing, a dialogue is going on inside you. You respond to some question buzzing around in your mind. The question might be "What was I thinking about when I did that?" or "How do I really feel about this?" In any case, most writing reacts to a question or a series of internal statements.

Sometimes, stating the questions explicitly and then answering them can help you understand what you are thinking about and feeling. When you write both the questions and your answers, you engage in a dialogue. All sorts of insights can result. You begin to see two sides of an issue. You take the part of someone else and view the matter at hand from her or his point of view. In short, you gain various perspectives. Helpful dialogue partners might be other people, the Father, Jesus, the Holy Spirit, your body, or your emotions.

Using a Prayer Journal

Many people write daily prayers to God as a way of keeping company with God. You can include numerous types of prayers in your journal: you can ask God for help or strength, express sorrow to the Lord about something, reflect on Scripture passages, give thanks and praise, and so on. However, a prayer journal does not have to be limited to forms of prayer such as these. Prayers can be any expression of what you want to say to God.

Saint Thérèse, the Little Flower

Saint Thérèse of Lisieux, the Little Flower, is among the most beloved of saints. She lived only a short time, yet her life gave testimony to the power of love. This testimony of God's love has been given to the world through her journal, *The Story of a Soul*.

Thérèse faced sorrow as a little girl when her mother died. Her family gathered around to help support her in her grief. Her father, "Papa," went with Thérèse on walks to a church where they prayed before the Eucharist every evening after school. Their walks and prayers together helped each heart heal as they grieved the loss of mother and wife.

At age nine, Thérèse experienced another loss. Her sister Pauline, her "second mother," left to join a convent. Thérèse felt shocked and abandoned, but before long, she said that she too would join the convent and did so at the age of fifteen.

Thérèse's spiritual life began to take her to something she called "the little way": loving God in the smallest of things. Through her journal, she realized powerful insights and new understandings of God. Today, hundreds of years after Thérèse's death, thousands of people have read her little way.

Live It!

Seek God's Help

Finally, before you begin writing, ask the Holy Spirit to use your journal to open your heart, eyes, and ears to the work of God in your life.

By continuing this particular journaling practice, you will begin to see ways that God works in your life. You will grow in understanding of how to listen. You will learn to recognize the events in your life that seem ordinary but are actually openings through which God is reaching out to you.

—THIS CHAPTER IS ADAPTED FROM CARL KOCH,
PRAYERWAYS, PP. 91–93

Part IV

LITURGICAL PRAYER

15 Liturgical Prayer

What do you know about your family history? Did your grandmother or grandfather ever show you photographs of their grandparents? As you looked at the pictures, did you realize that you resemble these people who share your DNA but who died long before you were born?

What do you know about your spiritual history? In the same way that your body shares DNA with your relatives, past and present, you also share a sort of spiritual DNA with people beyond your physical family. These people are your brothers and sisters, past and present, in Jesus Christ.

Gathering with the Church Present

When you gather with others for liturgical prayer—the Eucharist, the Liturgy of the Hours, the Sacrament of Penance and Reconciliation, the Sacrament of

Anointing of the Sick, and so forth—you gather with the people in your parish. But liturgical prayer is about gathering with so many more than those you see. You are gathering with Catholics in Kenya, Ireland, and Mexico. You are gathering with Catholics in Poland, Brazil, and Tanzania. Wherever the liturgy is celebrated, it is fundamentally the same. For example, did you know that no matter where in the world you go to Mass on a given Sunday, you would hear the same readings being read in your own parish? Well, you would, assuming you understood the language!

Gathering with the Church Past

Pick up an apple. A long time ago, someone planted apple seeds in an orchard. From one of those trees came hundreds of apples. The apple grower sold his apples, and

now people all over your area eat apples that came from the same tree as yours did. Imagine that you planted the seeds of your apple, grew an apple tree, and gave away your apples. Through your planting and giving, the circle that the original tree started has grown. And imagine that those people planted seeds and sold apples, and then those people did. Over the course of time, thousands of people would eat apples that came from the same tree.

In this analogy, the Last Supper is the apple tree. This is when Jesus "took a loaf of bread, and when he had given thanks, he broke it and gave it to them, saying, 'This is my body, which will be given for you; do this in memory of me'" (Luke 22:19). Something about that moment burned upon the hearts of the disciples.

The disciples continued this meal as Jesus commanded—"in remembrance." They went forth and began to evangelize and break bread with women and men who came to believe in Jesus. And for the past two thousand years, we have been receiving from the same tree.

When we gather at Mass, we gather with the disciples and with all those who have gone before us. We sit at the table of the Last Supper, and we "take" and "eat" (see Matthew 26:26). In this way, the Last Supper is never truly past but is always present, always among us.

Gathering to Become the Body of Christ

At every moment in the day, the Eucharistic liturgy is celebrated somewhere in the world. This celebration makes the past alive—the Last Supper is alive. At any celebration of the Eucharist, those who gather are transported in time and space. In the middle of a seemingly ordinary homily, in the middle of a ritual they have heard over and over again, in the middle of songs that may or may not be on key, all people are brought into the presence of the Risen Lord Jesus. He is real and he is there.

You gather with your present needs in your heart. At the Eucharist, you receive an invitation to bring your life, joys, pains, laughter, and sorrow and to join them to Jesus. You place yourself

Galatians—Diversity

into the bread and into the cup. Within the bread and cup, you find your brothers and sisters who have also placed themselves in the bread and cup, and you are united right then, in that moment.

The Eucharist is all about communion. You gather with your brothers and sisters all over the world. You gather with your sisters and brothers who gathered two thousand years ago. You gather to be in communion with God.

Communion, or "with union," is an interesting word for us Catholics. It describes the unity among us. It describes our relationship with God, and it describes the consecrated bread and wine that we receive when we come forward at the Eucharist.

But here is the mind-blowing thing: Catholics believe that the Communion we receive enables us to become the communion that we are called to—with God and with one another. In other words, the Body of Christ we hold in our hands gives us the grace to become the Body of Christ that is the Church, the home of God.

Come Early

Being early to a party can make many people feel self-conscious. At times like those, the early arrivals and the host may glance out the window, hoping someone else comes in, someone fun, someone familiar. There is usually the person who arrives fashionably late. Everyone is there, beginning to warm up to one another, when the life of the party shows up, and everyone else relaxes.

No doubt, the Eucharist is a celebration, but it is not a party. Come, and come early.

Take the moments before Mass to present yourself before God. Allow yourself time to pray and ask for God's will to be done in your life. Look at the altar and think about the great event that will happen in half an hour or so. Simply be at peace in God's presence.

Sometimes it is good to use your own words—no one knows your own heart better than you and God. Your words flow from your heart to God's.

Sometimes it is good to use other people's words, such as the prayers found in this book. In this way, you begin to experience the ancient nature of the Catholic faith. As you pray, think about the thousands of Catholics who have used the same words to lift their hearts to God.

The Eucharistic Liturgy: The Body of Christ Receives the Body of Christ to Become the Body of Christ

When we Catholics are called to the Eucharistic liturgy, we are called to participate with our hearts, minds, and bodies, or as the Church says, we are called to full, conscious, and active participation.

"But I don't get anything out of Mass!" This is a common regret many people, particularly young people, express. The Church calls us to extreme participation, but how can we fulfill that vision the Church holds?

In October 1962, Pope John XXIII gathered the leaders of the Church—cardinals, bishops, theologians, and philosophers—in Rome for the Second Vatican Council, saying that the Church needed a fresh approach to its timeless teachings.

When the council concluded in 1965, the council members defined that fresh approach for the Church and its members. In one of the writings from the council, a fresh approach was provided for the Eucharist.

Consider this excerpt from that writing:

> But in order that the Liturgy may be able to produce its full effects, it is necessary that the faithful come to it with proper dispositions, that their minds should be attuned to their voices, and that they should cooperate with divine grace lest they receive it in vain.[2] (*Constitution on the Sacred Liturgy* [*Sacrosanctum Concilium*, 1963], 11)

Proper Disposition

Though the term can sound vaguely scolding, having the *proper disposition* is pretty much key to learning anything. Have you ever been in a class with a know-it-all, someone who had an answer for everything? That person, no matter what the topic, always had "the exact same thing" happen to him or her. Annoying, isn't it? How much do you think that person is learning?

Having a proper disposition when you come to Mass simply means that you present yourself to God with an open heart. Rather than assuming the disposition of a know-it-all, you assume the disposition of a disciple. Your heart is focused on the God who calls you to come to the Eucharist, to communion with God and the Church. With your open heart focused on God, you are in a position to hear and respond to God.

Before going to church, here are some practical things you can do at home to help place you in the proper disposition:

- **Read the Scripture readings.** Refer to chapter 9, "Prayers That Express Our Love for God," in this book and use the *lectio divina* method of prayer with a Gospel or one of the other readings.

- **Look outside yourself.** Ask yourself two simple questions before you go to the Eucharist: Where has it been easy to see or feel the Lord during the past week? Where has it been hard to see or feel the Lord during the past week? The answers to such questions can open your heart to hearing God's voice at the liturgy.

- **Look inside yourself.** Consider your thoughts, words, and actions, the things you have done and the things you have failed to do. How have you been Christlike through the week? Give thanks for the ways you have been Christlike. Seek Jesus' help to be more like him in the ways that you haven't.

- **Look around yourself.** Consider the people you know and love. How do they need God's presence in their lives? Is someone sick? Is someone moving? Is someone worried and anxious? Bring those people within your heart to the Eucharist.

Minds Attuned to Voices

Have you ever been to Mass, listened to the Gospel reading, sat down to listen to the homily, and realized you can't remember what the Gospel reading was?

Your voice says amazing things during the Mass. Are you listening to what you are saying?

"I believe in one God, the Father, almighty, maker of heaven and earth, of all things visible and invisible."

"For the kingdom, the power, and the glory are yours, now and for ever."

"Lamb of God, you take away the sins of the world, have mercy on us."

—*Roman Missal*

If your mind is attuned to your voice, the words take on meaning. The prayers of the Mass become rich with meaning. At the sign of peace, you truly extend the peace of Christ when you greet the person next to you, rather than extending a weak "Hi, how are ya?" handshake.

During the Eucharist, you can fully, consciously, and actively participate. You can pray the words of the liturgy in the following ways:

- **Absorb the environment.** God comes to you through your senses. You see and hear God's word. You feel the embrace of God's love through friends and family. You smell Easter in the lilies. You touch your Baptism in the holy water. You are called to change your life in the purple of Lent. Engage your senses upon entering the Church and absorb the message of the Gospel.

- **At the gathering song, gather!** The opening song is intended to unite into one voice those who have gathered. Sing out. Listen to those around you. Praise God and begin to unify yourself with the people with whom you will soon commune.

- **Pay attention to the preparation of the gifts.** Sadly, the presentation of the bread and wine is often overshadowed by the collection of money. A good symbol is found in offering your money during that time, but don't stop there. Put yourself in the bread and cup. Because you have prepared yourself, you have something to offer. Join your hopes, work, prayers, concerns, hurts, worries, and every other part of yourself to the bread and cup. As these are changed into the Body and Blood of Christ, your life, too,

God . . . All in All

What does the Church ask of you at the Eucharist? How does God meet you at Mass? How are you called to participate? Consider the following words from the Church:

> The Church, therefore, earnestly desires that Christ's faithful, when present at this mystery of faith, should not be there as strangers or silent spectators; on the contrary, through a good understanding of the rites and prayers they should take part in the sacred action conscious of what they are doing, with devotion and full collaboration. They should be instructed by God's word and be nourished at the table of the Lord's body; they should give thanks to God; by offering the Immaculate Victim, not only through the hands of the priest, but also with him, they should learn also to offer themselves; through Christ the Mediator, they should be drawn day by day into ever more perfect union with God and with each other, so that finally God may be all in all. (*Constitution on the Sacred Liturgy*, 48)

Study It!

can be changed into the Body and Blood of Christ.

- **Make peace.** Sometimes when you go to the Eucharist, you may sit next to people, either family or friends, who have offended you or whom you have offended. The sign of peace before Communion is a time to make real peace with those people. Say "I'm sorry" or "I love you."

- **Receive in joy.** The greatest moment of unity in the liturgy is when everyone receives the Body and Blood of Christ. What a joyful moment! Take the sacred Body and precious Blood and know that you are in communion with the Body of Christ—Jesus himself and all members of his body.

Cooperate with Grace

The writings of the Second Vatican Council tell us that it is through the liturgy, especially the Eucharist, that "the work of our redemption is accomplished" (*Constitution on the Sacred Liturgy*, 2).

Much of Catholic life involves the visible and the invisible. The visible is both the means through which we receive grace and a reminder of the grace that God gives. The visible of the Mass is the Eucharist—the bread, which has become the Body of Christ, and the wine, which has become the Blood of Christ. The invisible is the grace that flows from the Body and Blood of Jesus Christ.

Through presenting yourself at Mass with a proper disposition, with your mind attuned to your voice, grace pours into your heart. Your soul becomes engaged by the power and love of God it receives. Your soul begins to respond; you feel a stirring toward something. The stirring shows itself in quiet ways. This stirring is given so that you may be the living presence of Jesus in the world and that you may continue to be changed into his Body and Blood. At the end of the liturgy, you are dismissed, sent to change and be changed. For example:

- **The Sacrament of Penance and Reconciliation.** Cooperating with divine grace means you go to Penance and Reconciliation. The work of being Christlike involves being honest, painfully honest. Where do

you offend God? How do you hurt others? When are you untrue to yourself? In Penance and Reconciliation, you are brought into harmony and your sins are forgiven.

- **Be light.** "The light shines in the darkness" (John 1:5) is a phrase from the Gospels that seems to jump out at you. To cooperate with divine grace means to be light to those who hurt and are in darkness—the darkness of depression or poverty, the darkness of sin or addiction. You are light.

You are part of the ever-singing song that is the Mass. You are in communion with all Catholics who were, who are, and who ever will be. This Holy and Sacred mystery cannot be understood with words but must be experienced in the heart. Come to Mass with the proper disposition, listen to your own voice, and cooperate with the divine grace offered to you.

Saint Augustine of Hippo

Saint Augustine was born in AD 354. You have probably heard many stories like his.

Augustine was raised by a Christian mother, who taught him about matters of faith. He went to a religious school and was a pretty good student. His father hoped to get enough money together to send Augustine to higher education, but it took awhile. During that time, Augustine got into all kinds of stuff. He was into the social scene big time. He got caught up in strange religions. He fathered a son with a woman who was not his wife. Augustine lived for nothing more than his personal enjoyment.

But then something happened. Through his mother's intervention and that of a bishop named Ambrose, Augustine returned to the faith of his childhood. He again embraced Christianity. Eventually he became a bishop and one of the greatest Christian thinkers.

Augustine loved words and philosophy. One of the phrases he made popular was *totus Christus*—the whole Christ. He saw that at the Eucharist, the whole Christ was made present and was unified. He defined the whole Christ as Jesus himself *and* all Christians. We are members of Christ himself.

At the Eucharist, this becomes a reality. At the Eucharist, Christians are united to Jesus and to one another, making one body and one spirit, receiving love from the Father and giving love back to the Father.

Live It!

16 A Four-Week Psalter

The Liturgy of the Hours is your prayer! It is the prayer the Church has given to all Christians. This is what the Church says to us about prayer:

> Jesus has commanded us to do as he did. On many occasions, he said: "pray" (Matthew 6:6), "ask" (Matthew 7:7), "in my name" (John 14:13).

We are the Body of Christ. We are his hands, his feet, and his voice. In the Liturgy of the Hours, we, as one member of the Body of Christ, join ourselves in spirit and voice to the entire Body of Christ throughout the world as we pray, ask, and seek with Jesus, our leader. Because it is the prayer of the Church, the Liturgy of the Hours is best prayed with others. We can also pray it alone, because it offers a good way to structure our daily prayer. We can join with friends to pray, when possible. Know, however, that when we pray alone, the saints and Christians throughout the world join us.

The Psalter provided here is an adaptation of this form of prayer, written especially for young people to use once a day. It is offered as an introduction to this form of prayer. The actual Liturgy of the Hours includes prayers for morning and evening, in a form that is similar to the one described here.

Structure of the Liturgy of the Hours

Call to Prayer

We make the Sign of the Cross and pray for God to be near us and help us as we continue our prayer.

God, come to my assistance.
Lord, make haste to help me.
Glory to the Father, and to the Son,
 and to the Holy Spirit:
as it was in the beginning, is now,
 and will be for ever. Amen.

Antiphon

Notice a phrase that is said before the Psalm and then repeated after it. This phrase is called the antiphon (AN-ti-fohn). It is said and then repeated to show the character of the Psalm or to highlight an important line in it that otherwise might be overlooked. By saying the antiphon in the beginning, we can know what is important in the Psalm. By saying it at the end, it reminds us of what we just prayed.

Psalm

The Psalms are God's Word. Humans wrote them under the inspiration of the Holy Spirit. They are a gift from God to us.

As people who have received God's blessings, we feel the need to praise and seek God or to ask for God's forgiveness. The Psalms are God's gift to us to help us voice our feelings to God.

The Psalms were Jesus' prayer book. They have been the Christian prayer book for two thousand years, and they remain the prayer book of Christians today. Imagine, every time we pray one of the Psalms, someone is praying them with us. We are joining our voice with countless Christians in making a gift to God.

Scripture Reading and Response to the Reading

Liturgical prayer is a conversation or a dialogue between God and God's people. God speaks. We listen. We respond. God listens. God responds. This is the pattern of the Liturgy of the Hours. We speak our feelings to God in the Psalm, and then God responds by speaking to us in the Scripture reading. Scripture is God's response to us as individuals and as a Church.

After we have heard God's voice, we again voice our feelings to God in the response to the reading.

Gospel Canticle and Antiphon

Three great hymns of praise appear in Luke's Gospel: the Canticle of Zechariah (1:68–79), the Canticle of Mary (1:46–55), and the Canticle of Simeon (2:29–32). All Scripture is inspired by the Holy Spirit, but Catholics hold the Gospels to be particularly important because they are the stories of Jesus. Because these hymns of praise are from the Gospels, Catholics pray them daily—the Canticle of Zechariah in the morning and the Canticle of Mary in the evening. The Canticle of Simeon is prayed at Night Prayers. You can find it and the Night Prayer Antiphon in chapter 2 of this book.

Petitions and the Lord's Prayer

As the dialogue with the Lord continues, we voice prayers in union with the whole Church, and we also have the chance to tell the Lord our needs and concerns. Then we draw all of the prayers, those from around the world and from our hearts, into the perfect prayer: the Lord's Prayer.

Closing Prayer and Dismissal

We conclude with a prayer that draws our conversation with the Lord to a close. But just as with any conversation with a friend, we leave God's presence having been changed.

Psalter Calendar

Praying the four-week Psalter is meant to simplify prayer, create an easy pattern for prayer, and create a rhythm for praying throughout your life. Knowing when to pray which prayers, however, can be confusing. Below is a guide for the years 2013 through 2016.

The four-week cycle of prayer simply repeats itself, but each liturgical season begins with week one. At times it may seem awkward, but just remember to go to week one whenever a new liturgical season starts.

Here is a word of caution. Do not get overly concerned with praying the right week at the right time. Just pray! The Liturgy of the Hours is an ancient prayer that has helped people meet the Lord throughout the centuries. Allow it to be a rhythm that can help establish a habit of daily prayer.

2013

First Sunday in Ordinary Time, January 13: Week 1

First Sunday of Lent, February 17: Week 1

Easter Sunday, March 31: Week 1

Pentecost Sunday, May 19: Week 3

First Sunday of Advent, December 1: Week 1

First Sunday of Christmas, December 29: Week 1

2014

First Sunday in Ordinary Time, January 12: Week 1

First Sunday of Lent, March 9: Week 1

Easter Sunday, April 20: Week 1

Pentecost Sunday, June 8: Week 2

First Sunday of Advent, November 30: Week 1

First Sunday of Christmas, December 28: Week 1

2015

First Sunday in Ordinary Time, January 11: Week 1

First Sunday of Lent, February 22: Week 1

Easter Sunday, April 5: Week 1
Pentecost Sunday, May 24: Week 4

First Sunday of Advent, November 29: Week 1

First Sunday of Christmas, December 27: Week 1

2016

First Sunday in Ordinary Time, January 10: Week 1

First Sunday of Lent, February 14: Week 1

Easter Sunday, March 27: Week 1

Pentecost Sunday, May 15: Week 3

First Sunday of Advent, November 27: Week 1

Christmas Day, December 25: Week 1

Call to Prayer

God, come to my assistance.
Lord, make haste to help me.
Glory to the Father, and to the
 Son, and to the Holy Spirit:
as it was in the beginning, is now,
 and will be for ever. Amen.

Psalm Antiphon

I am always safe with you, my
Lord; you are all I need in life.

Psalm 149

Praise the LORD!
Sing to the LORD a new song,
 his praise in the assembly of
 the faithful.
Let Israel be glad in its Maker;
 let the children of Zion rejoice
 in their King.
Let them praise his name with
 dancing,
 making melody to him with
 tambourine and lyre.
For the LORD takes pleasure in
 his people;
 he adorns the humble with
 victory.
Let the faithful exult in glory;
 let them sing for joy on their
 couches.

Let the high praises of God be in
 their throats
 and two-edged swords in their
 hands,
to execute vengeance on the
 nations
 and punishment on the
 peoples,
to bind their kings with fetters
 and their nobles with chains
 of iron,
to execute on them the judgment
 decreed.
 This is glory for all his faithful
 ones.
Praise the LORD!

Glory to the Father, and to the
 Son, and to the Holy Spirit:
as it was in the beginning, is now,
 and will be for ever. Amen.

Psalm Prayer

On this great day, we are filled
with joy as we celebrate your
Resurrection from the dead. May
the joy we feel carry us through
the week.

Psalm Antiphon

I am always safe with you, my
Lord; you are all I need in life.

Scripture Reading

So that you may not claim to be wiser than you are, brothers and sisters, I want you to understand this mystery: . . . Just as you were once disobedient to God but have now received mercy because of their disobedience, so they have now been disobedient in order that, by the mercy shown to you, they too may now receive mercy. For God has imprisoned all in disobedience so that he may be merciful to all.

O the depth of the riches and wisdom and knowledge of God! How unsearchable are his judgments and how inscrutable his ways!

"For who has known the mind
of the Lord?
Or who has been his
counselor?"
"Or who has given a gift to
him,
to receive a gift in return?"

For from him and through him and to him are all things. To him be the glory forever. Amen.

(ROMANS 11:25,30–36)

Prayer Response to the Reading

- My heart is filled with joy as I contemplate your works, O Lord.
- I celebrate the wisdom that brought all things into being, as I contemplate your works, O Lord.
- Glory to the Father, and to the Son, and to the Holy Spirit.
- My heart is filled with joy as I contemplate your works, O Lord.

Gospel Antiphon

It is the Lamb of God, who takes away the sins of the world.

Gospel Canticle

- If you are praying in the morning, pray the morning canticle found on page 249.
- If you are praying in the evening, pray the evening canticle found on page 250.

Glory to the Father, and to the
Son, and to the Holy Spirit:
as it was in the beginning, is now,
and will be for ever. Amen.

Gospel Antiphon
It is the Lamb of God, who takes away the sins of the world.

Petitions
Giving all glory and honor to the God who loves us, we ask for help as we pray: *Be with me, Lord.*

- God of mercy, shower the world with your love so that all may dwell in your peace, we pray. *Be with me, Lord.*

- God of compassion, look with kindness on those who are hurting, alone, and scared. Show them the compassion they need, we pray. *Be with me, Lord.*

- God of wisdom, guide the actions of those who lead us to words of peace and prosperity for all, we pray. *Be with me, Lord.*

- God of glory, reward with eternal life all those you have called to be with you, we pray. *Be with me, Lord.*

- God of strength, throughout the coming week, give us the strength to do what we know is right, we pray. *Be with me, Lord.*

- God of love, help us to answer your call to us and serve you with all of our hearts, we pray. *Be with me, Lord.*

Please take time to add your own needs and concerns.

Lord's Prayer
Let us pray in the perfect words taught to us by Jesus:
Our Father . . .

Closing Prayer
Always-present God, your watch reaches to all the ends of the earth. Even the pull of sin cannot stop your loving plans. Help us to receive your embrace and give us the strength to follow you and to reflect peace to those we meet. We ask this in the name of Jesus, the Lord, and with the power of the Holy Spirit. Amen.

Dismissal
May the Lord bless us and protect us from evil and bring us to the joy of Heaven. Amen.

Monday, Week 1

Call to Prayer

God, come to my assistance.
Lord, make haste to help me.
Glory to the Father, and to the
 Son, and to the Holy Spirit:
as it was in the beginning, is now,
 and will be for ever. Amen.

Psalm Antiphon

Worship the Lord in all his glory.

Psalm 29

Ascribe to the Lord, O heavenly
 beings,
 ascribe to the Lord glory and
 strength.
Ascribe to the Lord the glory of
 his name;
 worship the Lord in holy
 splendor.

The voice of the Lord is over
 the waters;
 the God of glory thunders,
 the Lord, over mighty waters.
The voice of the Lord is
 powerful;
 the voice of the Lord is full
 of majesty.

The voice of the Lord breaks
 the cedars;

the Lord breaks the cedars of
 Lebanon.
He makes Lebanon skip like
 a calf,
 and Sirion like a young
 wild ox.

The voice of the Lord flashes
 forth flames of fire.
The voice of the Lord shakes the
 wilderness;
 the Lord shakes the wilderness
 of Kadesh.

The voice of the Lord causes the
 oaks to whirl,
 and strips the forest bare;
 and in his temple all say,
 "Glory!"

The Lord sits enthroned over
 the flood;
 the Lord sits enthroned as
 king forever.
May the Lord give strength to
 his people!
 May the Lord bless his people
 with peace!

Glory to the Father, and to the
 Son, and to the Holy Spirit:
as it was in the beginning, is now,
 and will be for ever. Amen.

Psalm Prayer

Mighty God, your power is greater than any known in the world. Help us always to see your strength at work in the world, Lord, through others and through ourselves.

Psalm Antiphon

Worship the Lord in all his glory.

Scripture Reading

For this reason, since the day we heard it, we have not ceased praying for you and asking that you may be filled with the knowledge of God's will in all spiritual wisdom and understanding, so that you may lead lives worthy of the Lord, fully pleasing to him, as you bear fruit in every good work and as you grow in the knowledge of God. May you be made strong with all the strength that comes from his glorious power, and may you be prepared to endure everything with patience, while joyfully giving thanks to the Father, who has enabled you to share in the inheritance of the saints in the light. He has rescued us from the power of darkness and transferred us into the kingdom of his beloved Son.

(COLOSSIANS 1:9–13)

Prayer Response to the Reading

- Only you can rescue me, Lord, because my sins have brought you sadness.

- Please have mercy on me in my weakness, because my sins have brought you sadness.

- Glory to the Father, and to the Son, and to the Holy Spirit.

- Only you can rescue me, Lord, because my sins have brought you sadness.

Gospel Antiphon

Lord, if you will it, you can heal me. And Jesus said: "I do; you are healed."

Gospel Canticle

- If you are praying in the morning, pray the morning canticle found on page 249.

- If you are praying in the evening, pray the evening canticle found on page 250.

Glory to the Father, and to the
 Son, and to the Holy Spirit:
as it was in the beginning, is now,
 and will be for ever. Amen.

Gospel Antiphon

Lord, if you will it, you can heal
me. And Jesus said: "I do; you
are healed."

Petitions

God has made a covenant with us
that will never end. In gratitude
for all the gifts the Lord gives us,
we pray: *Lord, bless your people.*

- Give our leaders the wisdom
 and courage to make decisions
 for the good of all people, we
 pray. *Lord, bless your people.*

- Give those who hunger, food;
 those who hurt, comfort; and
 those who suffer, relief, we
 pray. *Lord, bless your people.*

- Give those who have died a
 place with you in Heaven, we
 pray. *Lord, bless your people.*

- Give us the courage to lead
 lives that are signs of you in
 this world, we pray. *Lord, bless
 your people.*

- Give us the patience to deal
 with the hassles that come

our way, we pray. *Lord, bless
your people.*

- Give our hearts the peace that
 only you can give us, we pray.
 Lord, bless your people.

*Please take time to add your own
needs and concerns.*

Lord's Prayer

Let us pray in the perfect words
taught to us by Jesus:
Our Father . . .

Closing Prayer

Heavenly Father, may our desire
to serve you bring us closer to
you. Hear the prayer of those
who work so hard to follow your
call in this world. Open all eyes
to see what is possible through
you. We ask this in the name of
Jesus, your Son and our Lord,
and with the power of the Holy
Spirit. Amen.

Dismissal

May the Lord bless us and pro-
tect us from evil and bring us to
the joy of Heaven. Amen.

Tuesday, Week 1

Call to Prayer

God, come to my assistance.
Lord, make haste to help me.
Glory to the Father, and to the
 Son, and to the Holy Spirit:
as it was in the beginning, is now,
 and will be for ever. Amen.

Psalm Antiphon

The one who has a pure and
humble heart will climb God's
mountain.

Psalm 24

The earth is the Lord's and all
 that is in it,
 the world, and those who live
 in it;
for he has founded it on the seas,
 and established it on the
 rivers.

Who shall ascend the hill of
 the Lord?
 And who shall stand in his
 holy place?
Those who have clean hands and
 pure hearts,
 who do not lift up their souls
 to what is false,
 and do not swear deceitfully.

They will receive blessing from
 the Lord,
 and vindication from the God
 of their salvation.
Such is the company of those
 who seek him,
 who seek the face of the God
 of Jacob.

Lift up your heads, O gates!
 and be lifted up, O ancient
 doors!
 that the King of glory may
 come in.
Who is the King of glory?
 The Lord, strong and mighty,
 the Lord, mighty in battle.
Lift up your heads, O gates!
 and be lifted up, O ancient
 doors!
 that the King of glory may
 come in.
Who is this King of glory?
 The Lord of hosts,
 he is the King of glory.

Glory to the Father, and to the
 Son, and to the Holy Spirit:
as it was in the beginning, is now,
 and will be for ever. Amen.

Psalm Prayer

Make us ready to welcome you when you come again in glory. Free us from sin, protect us from evil, and make us worthy to live forever in your presence.

Psalm Antiphon

The one who has a pure and humble heart will climb God's mountain.

Scripture Reading

See what love the Father has given us, that we should be called children of God; and that is what we are. The reason the world does not know us is that it did not know him. Beloved, we are God's children now; what we will be has not yet been revealed. What we do know is this: when he is revealed, we will be like him, for we will see him as he is. And all who have this hope in him purify themselves, just as he is pure.

(1 JOHN 3:1–3)

Prayer Response to the Reading

- Your promise to us remains strong forever.

- The New Covenant you made with us remains strong forever.
- Glory to the Father, and to the Son, and to the Holy Spirit.
- Your promise to us remains strong forever.

Gospel Antiphon

To truly be a child of God, pray for those who speak against you and your family.

Gospel Canticle

- If you are praying in the morning, pray the morning canticle found on page 249.
- If you are praying in the evening, pray the evening canticle found on page 250.

Glory to the Father, and to the Son, and to the Holy Spirit: as it was in the beginning, is now, and will be for ever. Amen.

Gospel Antiphon

To truly be a child of God, pray for those who speak against you and your family.

Petitions

Let us give praise to Christ, the Lord, who came to live among us and still does to this day as we pray: *Lord, hear our prayer.*

- Ruler of glory, show the rulers of our world how to rule with hearts of service, we pray. *Lord, hear our prayer.*

- Let daughters and sons learn from the example of your love and respect for your parents, we pray. *Lord, hear our prayer.*

- Free those trapped by oppression and hatred and guide them to the safety only you can bring, we pray. *Lord, hear our prayer.*

- Accept all who have left this world in your friendship and give them peace, we pray. *Lord, hear our prayer.*

- Make our hearts compassionate, as we struggle to be kind to those who hurt us, we pray. *Lord, hear our prayer.*

- Help us to know you and to love you in all we do and say, we pray. *Lord, hear our prayer.*

Please take time to add your own needs and concerns.

Lord's Prayer

Let us pray in the perfect words taught to us by Jesus:
Our Father . . .

Closing Prayer

Loving Father, thank you for the gift of being one of your children. May our prayers to you and our work in your name bring you joy and bring more people into your family of love. We ask this through our Lord, Jesus Christ, your Son, who lives and reigns with you in the unity of the Holy Spirit, one God, forever and ever. Amen.

Dismissal

May the Lord bless us and protect us from evil and bring us to the joy of Heaven. Amen.

Wednesday, Week 1

Call to Prayer

God, come to my assistance.
Lord, make haste to help me.
Glory to the Father, and to the
 Son, and to the Holy Spirit:
as it was in the beginning, is now,
 and will be for ever. Amen.

Psalm Antiphon

God is here, sing out in praise.

Psalm 47

Clap your hands, all you peoples;
 shout to God with loud songs
 of joy.
For the LORD, the Most High, is
 awesome,
 a great king over all the earth.
He subdued peoples under us,
 and nations under our feet.
He chose our heritage for us,
 the pride of Jacob whom he
 loves.

God has gone up with a shout,
 the LORD with the sound of
 a trumpet.
Sing praises to God, sing praises;
 sing praises to our King, sing
 praises.

For God is the king of all
 the earth;
 sing praises with a psalm.

God is king over the nations;
 God sits on his holy throne.
The princes of the peoples gather
 as the people of the God
 of Abraham.
For the shields of the earth
 belong to God;
 he is highly exalted.

Glory to the Father, and to the
 Son, and to the Holy Spirit:
as it was in the beginning, is now,
 and will be for ever. Amen.

Psalm Prayer

We celebrate your name as we sing
with all of our hearts. May our
voices always remember how you
brought us to a new life in you.

Psalm Antiphon

God is here, sing out in praise.

Scripture Reading

And what you hate, do not do to
anyone. . . . Give some of your
food to the hungry, and some of
your clothing to the naked. . . .

Seek advice from every wise person and do not despise any useful counsel. At all times bless the Lord God, and ask him that your ways may be made straight and that all your paths and plans may prosper.

(Tobit 4:15–16,18–19)

Prayer Response to the Reading

- Lead my heart closer to your will, my God.
- Guide my steps along the path, closer to your will, my God.
- Glory to the Father, and to the Son, and to the Holy Spirit.
- Lead my heart closer to your will, my God.

Gospel Antiphon

Seek the Kingdom of God first of all, and everything else will be given to you.

Gospel Canticle

- If you are praying in the morning, pray the morning canticle found on page 249.
- If you are praying in the evening, pray the evening canticle found on page 250.

Glory to the Father, and to the Son, and to the Holy Spirit: as it was in the beginning, is now, and will be for ever. Amen.

Gospel Antiphon

Seek the Kingdom of God first of all, and everything else will be given to you.

Petitions

In everything we do and say, God should be praised, because we are surrounded by his love. As chosen people, we pray: *Show us your love.*

- Remember your Church, the Church that wants nothing more than to see your face, we pray. *Show us your love.*
- Let all the countries come to see you as the one true path to happiness, we pray. *Show us your love.*
- Give our brothers and sisters all they truly need, we pray. *Show us your love.*
- Open the doors of Heaven to those who have passed on, and show them mercy, we pray. *Show us your love.*

- Keep us in the right path,
 and may our actions always be
 focused on you, we pray.
 Show us your love.

- Take away any anger and
 jealousy that leads us to hurt
 those around us, we pray.
 Show us your love.

*Please take time to add your own
needs and concerns.*

Lord's Prayer

Let us pray in the perfect words
taught to us by Jesus:
Our Father . . .

Closing Prayer

God, our provider, always watch
over us. In the middle of all that
burdens us in this life, give us
the strength and love to continue
using your name. We ask this
in the name of Jesus, the Lord,
and with the power of the Holy
Spirit. Amen.

Dismissal

May the Lord bless us and pro-
tect us from evil and bring us to
the joy of Heaven. Amen.

Thursday, Week 1

Call to Prayer

God, come to my assistance.
Lord, make haste to help me.
Glory to the Father, and to the
 Son, and to the Holy Spirit:
as it was in the beginning, is now,
 and will be for ever. Amen.

Psalm Antiphon

Sing out to our glorious God
in Heaven.

Psalm 57

Be merciful to me, O God, be
 merciful to me,
 for in you my soul takes refuge;
in the shadow of your wings
 I will take refuge,
 until the destroying storms
 pass by.
I cry to God Most High,
 to God who fulfills his
 purpose for me.
He will send from heaven and
 save me,
 he will put to shame those
 who trample on me.
God will send forth his steadfast
 love and his faithfulness.

I lie down among lions
 that greedily devour human prey;

their teeth are spears and arrows,
 their tongues sharp swords.

Be exalted, O God, above the
 heavens.
 Let your glory be over all the
 earth.

They set a net for my steps;
 my soul was bowed down.
They dug a pit in my path,
 but they have fallen into it
 themselves.
My heart is steadfast, O God,
 my heart is steadfast.
I will sing and make melody.
 Awake, my soul!
Awake, O harp and lyre!
 I will awake the dawn.
I will give thanks to you, O LORD,
 among the peoples;
 I will sing praises to you
 among the nations.
For your steadfast love is as high
 as the heavens;
 your faithfulness extends to
 the clouds.

Be exalted, O God, above the
 heavens.
 Let your glory be over all the
 earth.

Glory to the Father, and to the
Son, and to the Holy Spirit:
as it was in the beginning, is now,
and will be for ever. Amen.

Psalm Prayer

Rescue us from the grasping
hands of evil by showing to all
people your mercy and truth.
We can then spread your name
to all peoples as companions
on the journey.

Psalm Antiphon

Sing out to our glorious God
in Heaven.

Scripture Reading

In this you rejoice, even if now
for a little while you have had
to suffer various trials, so that
the genuineness of your faith—
being more precious than gold
that, though perishable, is tested
by fire—may be found to result
in praise and glory and honor
when Jesus Christ is revealed.
Although you have not seen
him, you love him; and even
though you do not see him now,
you believe in him and rejoice
with an indescribable and glori-
ous joy, for you are receiving the
outcome of your faith, the salva-
tion of your souls.

(1 PETER 1:6–9)

Prayer Response
to the Reading

- My heart cries out to you;
 hear my plea, O Lord.
- I will do what you ask of me,
 hear my plea, O Lord.
- Glory to the Father, and to the
 Son, and to the Holy Spirit.
- My heart cries out to you;
 hear my plea, O Lord.

Gospel Antiphon

Whoever does the will of God is
a true member of my family.

Gospel Canticle

- If you are praying in the
 morning, pray the morning
 canticle found on page 249.
- If you are praying in the eve-
 ning, pray the evening canticle
 found on page 250.

Glory to the Father, and to the
Son, and to the Holy Spirit:
as it was in the beginning, is now,
and will be for ever. Amen.

Gospel Antiphon

Whoever does the will of God is a true member of my family.

Petitions

All our hope is in our God, who gives us help. With this hope and faith, we pray: *Bless your children, O source of life.*

- Keep us always aware of the love you have for us and the works you do for us, we pray. *Bless your children, O source of life.*

- Let those who lead your Church bring us together and be your tools for good work, we pray. *Bless your children, O source of life.*

- As your children, give us patience with those who test our faith, we pray. *Bless your children, O source of life.*

- Take care of your children you have already brought into your loving presence, we pray. *Bless your children, O source of life.*

- Help us to keep a childlike heart and not let evil bring us down, we pray. *Bless your children, O source of life.*

- Give us the faith to serve you in the way you are calling us to serve, we pray. *Bless your children, O source of life.*

Please take time to add your own needs and concerns.

Lord's Prayer

Let us pray in the perfect words taught to us by Jesus:
Our Father . . .

Closing Prayer

Ancient of Days, we, your adopted sons and daughters, pray to you. Keep us safe in the darkness as we look for the light of truth, your Son, Jesus Christ, who lives and reigns with you and the Holy Spirit, one God, forever and ever. Amen.

Dismissal

May the Lord bless us and protect us from evil and bring us to the joy of Heaven. Amen.

Friday, Week 1

Call to Prayer

God, come to my assistance.
Lord, make haste to help me.
Glory to the Father, and to the
 Son, and to the Holy Spirit:
as it was in the beginning, is now,
 and will be for ever. Amen.

Psalm Antiphon

Go before our Lord and God
singing with happy hearts.

Psalm 51

Have mercy on me, O God,
 according to your steadfast love;
according to your abundant
 mercy
 blot out my transgressions.
Wash me thoroughly from my
 iniquity,
 and cleanse me from my sin.

For I know my transgressions,
 and my sin is ever before me.
Against you, you alone, have
 I sinned,
 and done what is evil in your
 sight,
so that you are justified in your
 sentence
 and blameless when you pass
 judgment.

Indeed, I was born guilty,
 a sinner when my mother
 conceived me.

You desire truth in the inward
 being;
 therefore teach me wisdom in
 my secret heart.
Purge me with hyssop, and I shall
 be clean;
 wash me, and I shall be whiter
 than snow.
Let me hear joy and gladness;
 let the bones that you have
 crushed rejoice.
Hide your face from my sins,
 and blot out all my iniquities.

Create in me a clean heart, O God,
 and put a new and right spirit
 within me.
Do not cast me away from your
 presence,
 and do not take your holy
 spirit from me.
Restore to me the joy of your
 salvation,
 and sustain in me a willing
 spirit.

Then I will teach transgressors
 your ways,
 and sinners will return to you.

Deliver me from bloodshed,
O God,
O God of my salvation,
and my tongue will sing aloud
of your deliverance.

O Lord, open my lips,
and my mouth will declare
your praise.
For you have no delight in
sacrifice;
if I were to give a burnt
offering, you would not
be pleased.
The sacrifice acceptable to God is
a broken spirit;
a broken and contrite heart, O
God, you will not despise.

Do good to Zion in your good
pleasure;
rebuild the walls of Jerusalem,
then you will delight in right
sacrifices,
in burnt offerings and whole
burnt offerings;
then bulls will be offered on
your altar.

Glory to the Father, and to the
Son, and to the Holy Spirit:
as it was in the beginning, is now,
and will be for ever. Amen.

Psalm Prayer

With all of our hearts, we call to
you and ask you to open our hearts
to announce your Good News.

Psalm Antiphon

Go before our Lord and God,
singing with happy hearts.

Scripture Reading

Let no evil talk come out of your
mouths, but only what is useful
for building up, as there is need,
so that your words may give grace
to those who hear. And do not
grieve the Holy Spirit of God,
with which you were marked
with a seal for the day of redemp-
tion. Put away from you all bit-
terness and wrath and anger and
wrangling and slander, together
with all malice, and be kind to
one another, tenderhearted, for-
giving one another, as God in
Christ has forgiven you.

(EPHESIANS 4:29–32)

Prayer Response
to the Reading

- Christ forgives us and cleanses
 us of our sins with his blood.

- A nation of people to lead and
 serve, with his blood.

- Glory to the Father, and to the Son, and to the Holy Spirit.
- Christ forgives us and cleanses us of our sins with his blood.

Gospel Antiphon

Whatever it is you do, do it in the name of Jesus Christ.

Gospel Canticle

- If you are praying in the morning, pray the morning canticle found on page 249.
- If you are praying in the evening, pray the evening canticle found on page 250.

Glory to the Father, and to the Son, and to the Holy Spirit:
as it was in the beginning, is now, and will be for ever. Amen.

Gospel Antiphon

Whatever it is you do, do it in the name of Jesus Christ.

Petitions

Through the Cross, Jesus brought salvation to the people. In amazement at this selfless act, we pray: *Be with me, Lamb of God.*

- Upon the Cross, Jesus offered the perfect sacrifice, so for all those who suffer without God's love, we pray. *Be with me, Lamb of God.*
- Set free those unjustly imprisoned. Bring to good health those who are sick and injured, we pray. *Be with me, Lamb of God.*
- Cover us, your people, in the armor of salvation that protects us from the deceptions of sin, we pray. *Be with me, Lamb of God.*
- Lead the departed into the light of your dwelling place to look upon you forever, we pray. *Be with me, Lamb of God.*
- Help us see that the Lord is at our side in the struggles and problems of our daily life, we pray. *Be with me, Lamb of God.*
- May our words build up our friends and family and not drag them down, we pray. *Be with me, Lamb of God.*

Please take time to add your own needs and concerns.

Lord's Prayer

Let us pray in the perfect words taught to us by Jesus:
Our Father . . .

Closing Prayer

God, our source of life, help us
to follow the example of Jesus,
sharing the burden he carries for
us, bearing all wrongs patiently.
Through these acts, may we
come to share in his glory in the
Kingdom where he lives with you
and the Holy Spirit, one God,
forever and ever. Amen.

Dismissal

May the Lord bless us and pro-
tect us from evil and bring us to
the joy of Heaven. Amen.

Call to Prayer

God, come to my assistance.
Lord, make haste to help me.
Glory to the Father, and to the
 Son, and to the Holy Spirit:
as it was in the beginning, is now,
 and will be for ever. Amen.

Psalm Antiphon

Blessed are you, Mary ever virgin,
for you carried the Creator of the
world in your womb.

Psalm 113

Praise the LORD!
Praise, O servants of the LORD;
 praise the name of the LORD.

Blessed be the name of the LORD
 from this time on and
 forevermore.
From the rising of the sun to
 its setting
 the name of the LORD is to
 be praised.
The LORD is high above all nations,
 and his glory above the heavens.

Who is like the LORD our God,
 who is seated on high,
who looks far down
 on the heavens and the earth?

He raises the poor from the dust,
 and lifts the needy from the
 ash heap,
to make them sit with princes,
 with the princes of his people.
He gives the barren woman a
 home,
 making her the joyous mother
 of children.
Praise the LORD!

Glory to the Father, and to the
 Son, and to the Holy Spirit:
as it was in the beginning, is now,
 and will be for ever. Amen.

Psalm Prayer

The Mighty One was blessed by
Mary's act of trust and love. We
pray that our actions in our lives
can also praise the Lord our God.

Psalm Antiphon

Blessed are you, Mary ever virgin,
for you carried the Creator of the
world in your womb.

Scripture Reading

I will greatly rejoice in the LORD,
 my whole being shall exult in
 my God;

for he has clothed me with the
garments of salvation,
he has covered me with the
robe of righteousness,
as a bridegroom decks himself
with a garland,
and as a bride adorns herself
with her jewels.

(ISAIAH 61:10)

Prayer Response to the Reading

- Hail Mary, full of grace, the Lord is with you.
- Blessed are you among women, and blessed is the fruit of your womb. The Lord is with you.
- Glory to the Father, and to the Son, and to the Holy Spirit.
- Hail Mary, full of grace, the Lord is with you.

Gospel Antiphon

You are the glory of Jerusalem, the joy of Israel, the most honored of your people.

Gospel Canticle

- If you are praying in the morning, pray the morning canticle found on page 249.

- If you are praying in the evening, pray the evening canticle found on page 250.

Glory to the Father, and to the Son, and to the Holy Spirit:
as it was in the beginning, is now, and will be for ever. Amen.

Gospel Antiphon

You are the glory of Jerusalem, the joy of Israel, the most honored of your people.

Petitions

Let us give thanks to Jesus, our Savior, who chose the Virgin Mary for his Mother. With courage, we pray: *May your Mother intercede for us, Jesus, our Savior.*

- By your redeeming power, you preserved your Mother from all stain of sin. Keep watch over your people and lead us from sin, we pray. *May your Mother intercede for us, Jesus, our Savior.*

- Mary was pure and immaculate as the sanctuary of the Holy Spirit. Help to make us worthy of your gifts, we pray. *May your Mother intercede for us, Jesus, our Savior.*

- You taught Mary to choose your will. Give us the wisdom to imitate her perfect example, we pray. *May your Mother intercede for us, Jesus, our Savior.*

- You crowned Mary as Queen of Heaven and set her next to you. Grant us a share in this glory, we pray. *May your Mother intercede for us, Jesus, our Savior.*

- Mary did not let her world influence her decision to be your Mother. Give us the courage not to let our world influence us in serving you, we pray. *May your Mother intercede for us, Jesus, our Savior.*

- Though very young, Mary responded when you called. Help us to respond to you and not let our age or other concerns worry us, we pray. *May your Mother intercede for us, Jesus, our Savior.*

Please take time to add your own needs and concerns.

Lord's Prayer

Let us pray in the perfect words taught to us by Jesus:
Our Father . . .

Closing Prayer

God of mercy, give us strength. May we who honor the memory of the Mother of God rise above the sins and failings of the past with the help of her prayers and example. Grant this through our Lord, Jesus Christ, your Son, who lives and reigns with you and the Holy Spirit, one God, forever and ever. Amen.

Dismissal

May the Lord bless us and protect us from evil and bring us to the joy of Heaven. Amen.

Call to Prayer

God, come to my assistance.
Lord, make haste to help me.
Glory to the Father, and to the
 Son, and to the Holy Spirit:
as it was in the beginning, is now,
 and will be for ever. Amen.

Psalm Antiphon

Praise the Lord's never-ending
greatness in song.

Psalm 150

Praise the Lord!
Praise God in his sanctuary;
 praise him in his mighty
 firmament!
Praise him for his mighty deeds;
 praise him according to his
 surprising greatness!

Praise him with trumpet sound;
 praise him with lute and harp!
Praise him with tambourine
 and dance;
 praise him with strings and
 pipe!
Praise him with clanging cymbals;
 praise him with loud clashing
 cymbals!

Let everything that breathes
 praise the Lord!
Praise the Lord!

Glory to the Father, and to the
 Son, and to the Holy Spirit:
as it was in the beginning, is now,
 and will be for ever. Amen.

Psalm Prayer

God of triumph, everything you
do is worthy of our thanks and
praise. May all our songs be sung
from our hearts and be just the
beginning of endless gratitude for
your love.

Psalm Antiphon

Praise the Lord's never-ending
greatness in song.

Scripture Reading

I will sprinkle clean water upon
you, and you shall be clean from
all your uncleannesses, and from
all your idols I will cleanse you. A
new heart I will give you, and a
new spirit I will put within you;
and I will remove from your body
the heart of stone and give you a
heart of flesh. And I will put my

spirit within you, and make you follow in my statutes and be careful to observe my ordinances. Then you shall live in the land that I gave to your ancestors; and you shall be my people, and I will be your God.

(Ezekiel 36:25–28)

Prayer Response to the Reading

- Give me a heart pure and clean, my God.
- In place of a heart hardened by hate and sin, pure and clean, my God.
- Glory to the Father, and to the Son, and to the Holy Spirit.
- Give me a heart pure and clean, my God.

Gospel Antiphon

Where you keep your treasures, you also keep your heart.

Gospel Canticle

- If you are praying in the morning, pray the morning canticle found on page 249.
- If you are praying in the evening, pray the evening canticle found on page 250.

Glory to the Father, and to the Son, and to the Holy Spirit: as it was in the beginning, is now, and will be for ever. Amen.

Gospel Antiphon

Where you keep your treasures, you also keep your heart.

Petitions

Let us praise and honor Jesus, our Savior, who died and rose again in glory. Praising him, let us pray: *Raise us up, victorious Savior.*

- Give guidance to those who lead your Church in word and action and lift them up as an example for all, we pray. *Raise us up, victorious Savior.*
- Give peace to those who are sick and suffering and help them rise above their weaknesses, we pray. *Raise us up, victorious Savior.*
- Give faith to those who do not believe in your boundless love and bring them up from the fear and confusion that keeps them down, we pray. *Raise us up, victorious Savior.*
- Give patience to us this week as we try to live as you called

us and lift us above all that may get in our way, we pray. *Raise us up, victorious Savior.*

- Give healing to those we may have hurt with our own words and actions and pull us up from our sinful ways, we pray. *Raise us up, victorious Savior.*

- Give mercy to those who have died and raise them up on the last day, we pray. *Raise us up, victorious Savior.*

Please take time to add your own needs and concerns.

Lord's Prayer

Let us pray in the perfect words taught to us by Jesus:
Our Father . . .

Closing Prayer

Almighty Father, your love is more than we can ever imagine. Fill our hearts with your love, our thoughts with your wisdom, and our mouths with your words, so that our entire lives may be a part of your plan. We ask this in the name of Jesus, the Lord, and with the power of the Holy Spirit. Amen.

Dismissal

May the Lord bless us and protect us from evil and bring us to the joy of Heaven. Amen.

Monday, Week 2

Call to Prayer

God, come to my assistance.
Lord, make haste to help me.
Glory to the Father, and to the
 Son, and to the Holy Spirit:
as it was in the beginning, is now,
 and will be for ever. Amen.

Psalm Antiphon

All of Heaven echoes with your
praises, O Lord.

Psalm 19:1–6

The heavens are telling the glory
 of God;
 and the firmament proclaims
 his handiwork.
Day to day pours forth speech,
 and night to night declares
 knowledge.
There is no speech, nor are there
 words;
 their voice is not heard;
yet their voice goes out through
 all the earth,
 and their words to the end of
 the world.

In the heavens he has set a tent
 for the sun,
which comes out like a bridegroom
 from his wedding canopy,

and like a strong man runs its
 course with joy.
Its rising is from the end of the
 heavens,
 and its circuit to the end of
 them;
 and nothing is hid from its heat.

Glory to the Father, and to the
 Son, and to the Holy Spirit:
as it was in the beginning, is now,
 and will be for ever. Amen.

Psalm Prayer

Glorious God, all you have done
for your people is amazing and
beyond approach. May we always
honor your love for us with praise
of your name.

Psalm Antiphon

All of Heaven echoes with your
praises, O Lord.

Scripture Reading

As you know, we dealt with each
one of you like a father with his
children, urging and encouraging you and pleading that you
lead a life worthy of God, who
calls you into his own kingdom
and glory.

We also constantly give thanks to God for this, that when you received the Word of God that you heard from us, you accepted it not as a human word but as what it really is, God's word, which is also at work in you believers.

(1 Thessalonians 2:11–13)

Prayer Response to the Reading

- Lord, hear my prayer that rises up to you.
- Like incense burning before you, that rises up to you.
- Glory to the Father, and to the Son, and to the Holy Spirit.
- Lord, hear my prayer that rises up to you.

Gospel Antiphon

A great prophet has come to us, and God is in our midst.

Gospel Canticle

- If you are praying in the morning, pray the morning canticle found on page 249.
- If you are praying in the evening, pray the evening canticle found on page 250.

Glory to the Father, and to the Son, and to the Holy Spirit: as it was in the beginning, is now, and will be for ever. Amen.

Gospel Antiphon

A great prophet has come to us, and God is in our midst.

Petitions

Our Savior has made us holy, a people set apart to do his will. With that in mind, we call out in prayer: *Hear your people, O Holy One.*

- Remember your Church throughout the world and continue to bless it and keep it safe, we pray. *Hear your people, O Holy One.*
- Take care of the poor, the suffering, and those who are forced to go without basic needs, we pray. *Hear your people, O Holy One.*
- Move the hearts of those who refuse to know your love and compassion, we pray. *Hear your people, O Holy One.*
- Enable us to see you in others, even when they are least like you, we pray. *Hear your people, O Holy One.*

- Take our daily efforts to serve you as our prayer of thanks, we pray. *Hear your people, O Holy One.*

- Lead all souls to your heavenly Kingdom, especially those most in need of your care, we pray. *Hear your people, O Holy One.*

Please take time to add your own needs and concerns.

Lord's Prayer

Let us pray in the perfect words taught to us by Jesus:
Our Father . . .

Closing Prayer

Father, you have blessed us with the opportunity to do your work. Give us what we need, keep us safe, and see what we do as honoring you for all you have done for us. We ask this through our Lord, Jesus Christ, your Son, who lives and reigns with you, in the unity of the Holy Spirit, one God, forever and ever. Amen.

Dismissal

May the Lord bless us and protect us from evil and bring us to the joy of Heaven. Amen.

Tuesday, Week 2

Call to Prayer

God, come to my assistance.
Lord, make haste to help me.
Glory to the Father, and to the
 Son, and to the Holy Spirit:
as it was in the beginning, is now,
 and will be for ever. Amen.

Psalm Antiphon

You have come to the earth and
showered it with your rain to
bring forth its bounty.

Psalm 65

Praise is due to you,
 O God, in Zion;
and to you shall vows be performed,
 O you who answer prayer!
To you all flesh shall come.
When deeds of iniquity
 overwhelm us,
 you forgive our transgressions.
Happy are those whom you choose
 and bring near
 to live in your courts.
We shall be satisfied with the
 goodness of your house,
 your holy temple.

By awesome deeds you answer us
 with deliverance,
 O God of our salvation;

you are the hope of all the ends
 of the earth
 and of the farthest seas.
By your strength you established
 the mountains;
 you are girded with might.
You silence the roaring of the seas,
 the roaring of their waves,
 the tumult of the peoples.
Those who live at earth's farthest
 bounds are awed by
 your signs;
you make the gateways of the
 morning and the evening
 shout for joy.

You visit the earth and water it,
 you greatly enrich it;
the river of God is full of water;
 you provide the people with
 grain,
 for so you have prepared it.
You water its furrows abundantly,
 settling its ridges,
softening it with showers,
 and blessing its growth.
You crown the year with your
 bounty;
 your wagon tracks overflow
 with richness.
The pastures of the wilderness
 overflow,

the hills gird themselves with joy,
the meadows clothe themselves
 with flocks,
 the valleys deck themselves
 with grain,
 they shout and sing together
 for joy.

Glory to the Father, and to the
 Son, and to the Holy Spirit:
as it was in the beginning, is now,
 and will be for ever. Amen.

Psalm Prayer

Like rain, pour your spirit out
upon us, Lord, and bless the fruit
of our work. Hear our prayer and
our praise of your name.

Psalm Antiphon

You have come to the earth and
showered it with your rain to
bring forth its bounty.

Scripture Reading

For you yourselves know very
well that the day of the Lord
will come like a thief in the
night. When they say, "There is
peace and security," then sudden
destruction will come upon them,
as labor pains come upon a preg-
nant woman, and there will be no
escape! But you, beloved, are not
in darkness, for that day to sur-
prise you like a thief; for you are
all children of light and children
of the day; we are not of the night
or of darkness. So then let us not
fall asleep as others do, but let us
keep awake and be sober.

(1 Thessalonians 5:2–6)

Prayer Response to the Reading

- I will know what true happi-
ness is when I see you face-to-
face, my Lord.
- Contentment and never-ending
peace with you, when I see
you face-to-face, my Lord.
- Glory to the Father, and to the
Son, and to the Holy Spirit.
- I will know what true happi-
ness is when I see you face-to-
face, my Lord.

Gospel Antiphon

When the Son of Man comes
among us, will he find faith in
our hearts?

Gospel Canticle

- If you are praying in the
morning, pray the morning
canticle found on page 249.

- If you are praying in the evening, pray the evening canticle found on page 250.

Glory to the Father, and to the
 Son, and to the Holy Spirit:
as it was in the beginning, is now,
 and will be for ever. Amen.

Gospel Antiphon

When the Son of Man comes among us, will he find faith in our hearts?

Petitions

The Lord, our God, is the hope of the earth, hearing our prayers and praises. It is with this hope that we pray: *Lord, hear our prayer.*

- Guide the minds of world leaders to actions that will benefit all peoples, we pray. *Lord, hear our prayer.*

- Guide the hands of your sons and daughters to work for your glory and praise, we pray. *Lord, hear our prayer.*

- Guide the mouths of those who hate to speak words of kindness and forgiveness, we pray. *Lord, hear our prayer.*

- Guide our ears to hear you calling to us in the everyday events of our lives, we pray. *Lord, hear our prayer.*

- Guide the eyes of all to see you in all your glory, we pray. *Lord, hear our prayer.*

- Guide those who have left this world in your friendship into the true happiness of your presence, we pray. *Lord, hear our prayer.*

Please take time to add your own needs and concerns.

Lord's Prayer

Let us pray in the perfect words taught to us by Jesus:
Our Father . . .

Closing Prayer

Almighty God, we await your return by continuing to do your will. Help us always to praise you and bless you in all we do and say. Remember our successes and forgive our failures. We ask this in the name of Jesus, the Lord, and in the power of the Holy Spirit. Amen.

Dismissal

May the Lord bless us and protect us from evil and bring us to the joy of Heaven. Amen.

Wednesday, Week 2

Call to Prayer

God, come to my assistance.
Lord, make haste to help me.
Glory to the Father, and to the
 Son, and to the Holy Spirit:
as it was in the beginning, is now,
 and will be for ever. Amen.

Psalm Antiphon

The Lord rules all the earth, let
all people be glad.

Psalm 97

The LORD is king! Let the earth
 rejoice;
 let the many coastlands be
 glad!
Clouds and thick darkness are all
 around him;
 righteousness and justice are
 the foundation of his throne.
Fire goes before him,
 and consumes his adversaries
 on every side.
His lightnings light up the world;
 the earth sees and trembles.
The mountains melt like wax
 before the LORD,
 before the LORD of all the earth.

The heavens proclaim his
 righteousness;

and all the peoples behold his
 glory.
All worshipers of images are put
 to shame,
 those who make their boast in
 worthless idols;
 all gods bow down before him.
Zion hears and is glad,
 and the towns of Judah rejoice,
 because of your judgments,
 O God.
For you, O LORD, are most high
 over all the earth;
 you are exalted far above all gods.

The LORD loves those who hate
 evil;
 he guards the lives of his
 faithful;
 he rescues them from the
 hand of the wicked.
Light dawns for the righteous,
 and joy for the upright in
 heart.
Rejoice in the LORD, O you
 righteous,
 and give thanks to his holy
 name!

Glory to the Father, and to the
 Son, and to the Holy Spirit:
as it was in the beginning, is now,
 and will be for ever. Amen.

Psalm Prayer

Father, we see your incredible power in the world you created and your incredible love in the way you treat your sons and daughters. Do not forget your love for us and continue to give us everything we need today, tomorrow, and forever.

Psalm Antiphon

The Lord rules all the earth, let all people be glad.

Scripture Reading

Who will separate us from the love of Christ? Will hardship, or distress, or persecution, or famine, or nakedness, or peril, or sword? As it is written,

"For your sake we are being killed all day long;
we are accounted as sheep to be slaughtered."

No, in all these things we are more than conquerors through him who loved us. For I am convinced that neither death, nor life, nor angels, nor rulers, nor things present, nor things to come, nor powers, nor height, nor depth, nor anything else in all creation, will be able to separate us from the love of God in Christ Jesus our Lord.

(ROMANS 8:35–39)

Prayer Response to the Reading

- I will praise the name of the Lord all the days of my life.
- From my mouth a song of praise, all the days of my life.
- Glory to the Father, and to the Son, and to the Holy Spirit.
- I will praise the name of the Lord all the days of my life.

Gospel Antiphon

Your strong arm scatters the prideful, and lifts up the humble.

Gospel Canticle

- If you are praying in the morning, pray the morning canticle found on page 249.
- If you are praying in the evening, pray the evening canticle found on page 250.

Glory to the Father, and to the Son, and to the Holy Spirit:
as it was in the beginning, is now, and will be for ever. Amen.

Gospel Antiphon

Your strong arm scatters the prideful, and lifts up the humble.

Petitions

Let us rejoice in God, for his pleasure comes from using his power to benefit his people. With this on our hearts, we pray: *Strengthen your people, God, our Savior.*

- Build up the faith of your people on earth, giving them hearts of service and minds always focused on you, we pray. *Strengthen your people, God, our Savior.*

- Give grace to the weak in mind, body, and spirit to overcome things that cause pain, we pray. *Strengthen your people, God, our Savior.*

- Protect all nature and all your creation from those who would harm it, we pray. *Strengthen your people, God, our Savior.*

- Grant us the ability to stand up for what we know is right and help us to live uprightly in what we say and do, we pray. *Strengthen your people, God, our Savior.*

- Use our daily actions as examples for others so they may see your goodness, we pray. *Strengthen your people, God, our Savior.*

- Give those who have gone before us a place with you in Heaven, we pray. *Strengthen your people, God, our Savior.*

Please take time to add your own needs and concerns.

Lord's Prayer

Let us pray in the perfect words taught to us by Jesus:
Our Father . . .

Closing Prayer

Heavenly Father, you want nothing else but for us to be happy, and that happiness can be found only with you. Recognize our efforts this day to come closer to you and do not hold our setbacks against us. We ask this through our Lord, Jesus Christ, your Son, who lives and reigns with you, in the unity of the Holy Spirit, one God, forever and ever. Amen.

Dismissal

May the Lord bless us and protect us from evil and bring us to the joy of Heaven. Amen.

Thursday, Week 2

Call to Prayer

God, come to my assistance.
Lord, make haste to help me.
Glory to the Father, and to the
 Son, and to the Holy Spirit:
as it was in the beginning, is now,
 and will be for ever. Amen.

Psalm Antiphon

Sing out in joy to God who is the
strength of his people.

Psalm 81

Sing aloud to God our strength;
 shout for joy to the God
 of Jacob.
Raise a song, sound the tambourine,
 the sweet lyre with the harp.
Blow the trumpet at the new
 moon,
 at the full moon, on our festal
 day.
For it is a statute for Israel,
 an ordinance of the God of
 Jacob.
He made it a decree in Joseph,
 when he went out over the
 land of Egypt.

I hear a voice I had not known:
"I relieved your shoulder of
 the burden;
 your hands were freed from
 the basket.
In distress you called, and I
 rescued you;
 I answered you in the secret
 place of thunder;
 I tested you at the waters of
 Meribah.

Hear, O my people, while I
 admonish you;
 O Israel, if you would but
 listen to me!
There shall be no strange god
 among you;
 you shall not bow down to a
 foreign god.
I am the LORD your God,
 who brought you up out of
 the land of Egypt.
 Open your mouth wide and
 I will fill it.

"But my people did not listen
 to my voice;
 Israel would not submit to me.
So I gave them over to their
 stubborn hearts,
 to follow their own counsels.
O that my people would listen
 to me,
 that Israel would walk in
 my ways!

Then I would quickly subdue
 their enemies,
 and turn my hand against
 their foes.
Those who hate the LORD would
 cringe before him,
 and their doom would last
 forever.
I would feed you with the finest
 of the wheat,
 and with honey from the rock
 I would satisfy you."

Glory to the Father, and to the
 Son, and to the Holy Spirit:
as it was in the beginning, is now,
 and will be for ever. Amen.

Psalm Prayer

Open our hearts, Lord, so that we
can give you praise. Help us leave
the temptation of sin behind and
fill our lives with your love.

Psalm Antiphon

Sing out in joy to God who is the
strength of his people.

Scripture Reading

So then, each of us will be account-
able to God.

 Let us therefore no longer pass
judgment on one another, but
resolve instead never to put a stum-
bling block or hindrance in the way
of another. . . . For the kingdom
of God is not food and drink but
righteousness and peace and joy in
the Holy Spirit. The one who thus
serves Christ is acceptable to God
and has human approval. Let us
then pursue what makes for peace
and for mutual upbuilding.

(ROMANS 14:12–13,17–19)

Prayer Response to the Reading

- Go out and tell all the world
 how wonderful God has been.

- Make known the blessings to
 all people how wonderful God
 has been.

- Glory to the Father, and to the
 Son, and to the Holy Spirit.

- Go out and tell all the world
 how wonderful God has been.

Gospel Antiphon

If you want holiness, God can give
you what you need, and more.

Gospel Canticle

- If you are praying in the
 morning, pray the morning
 canticle found on page 249.

- If you are praying in the eve-
 ning, pray the evening canticle
 found on page 250.

Glory to the Father, and to the
Son, and to the Holy Spirit:
as it was in the beginning, is now,
and will be for ever. Amen.

Gospel Antiphon

If you want holiness, God can give
you what you need, and more.

Petitions

Lift up your hearts to the Lord
and give thanks for his many
mercies and blessings. In this
spirit of affection, we pray: *Have
mercy and hear us.*

- Strengthen the Pope and bish-
 ops, who lead your people, and
 keep them safe from any harm,
 we pray. *Have mercy and hear us.*

- Protect our brothers and sis-
 ters who have no one to care
 for them and are in troubled
 situations, we pray. *Have
 mercy and hear us.*

- Take care of our friends and
 families that are far away from
 us and keep them safe until we
 can see them again, we pray.
 Have mercy and hear us.

- Direct our thoughts, feelings,
 and actions this day and always
 and help us follow your call, we
 pray. *Have mercy and hear us.*

- Show those who do not know
 your love the peace that comes
 with your name, we pray.
 Have mercy and hear us.

- Raise those who have died and
 bring them into your everlast-
 ing glory, we pray. *Have mercy
 and hear us.*

*Please take time to add your own
needs and concerns.*

Lord's Prayer

Let us pray in the perfect words
taught to us by Jesus:
Our Father . . .

Closing Prayer

Father of all, you constantly
call us to serve you in the world
around us. Help us always to do
our best to honor you in all we
do and in those we meet. We
ask this through our Lord, Jesus
Christ, your Son, who lives and
reigns with you, in the unity of
the Holy Spirit, one God, forever
and ever. Amen.

Dismissal

May the Lord bless us and pro-
tect us from evil and bring us to
the joy of Heaven. Amen.

Friday, Week 2

Call to Prayer

God, come to my assistance.
Lord, make haste to help me.
Glory to the Father, and to the
 Son, and to the Holy Spirit:
as it was in the beginning, is now,
 and will be for ever. Amen.

Psalm Antiphon

God will not reject a humble,
sincere heart.

Psalm 51

Have mercy on me, O God,
 according to your steadfast love;
according to your abundant mercy
 blot out my transgressions.
Wash me thoroughly from my
 iniquity,
 and cleanse me from my sin.

For I know my transgressions,
 and my sin is ever before me.
Against you, you alone, have
 I sinned,
 and done what is evil in your
 sight,
so that you are justified in your
 sentence
 and blameless when you pass
 judgment.

Indeed, I was born guilty,
 a sinner when my mother
 conceived me.

You desire truth in the inward
 being;
 therefore teach me wisdom in
 my secret heart.
Purge me with hyssop, and I shall
 be clean;
 wash me, and I shall be whiter
 than snow.
Let me hear joy and gladness;
 let the bones that you have
 crushed rejoice.
Hide your face from my sins,
 and blot out all my iniquities.

Create in me a clean heart, O God,
 and put a new and right spirit
 within me.
Do not cast me away from your
 presence,
 and do not take your holy
 spirit from me.
Restore to me the joy of your
 salvation,
 and sustain in me a willing
 spirit.

Then I will teach transgressors
 your ways,
 and sinners will return to you.

Deliver me from bloodshed,
 O God,
 O God of my salvation,
 and my tongue will sing aloud
 of your deliverance.

O Lord, open my lips,
 and my mouth will declare
 your praise.
For you have no delight in
 sacrifice;
 if I were to give a burnt
 offering, you would not
 be pleased.
The sacrifice acceptable to God
 is a broken spirit;
 a broken and contrite heart,
 O God, you will not
 despise.

Do good to Zion in your good
 pleasure;
 rebuild the walls of Jerusalem,
then you will delight in right
 sacrifices,
 in burnt offerings and whole
 burnt offerings;
 then bulls will be offered on
 your altar.

Glory to the Father, and to the
 Son, and to the Holy Spirit:
as it was in the beginning, is now,
 and will be for ever. Amen.

Psalm Prayer

Father, see our intention to love
you as sincere and do not reject
us in our weakness. You are the
Good News for which we long.

Psalm Antiphon

God will not reject a humble,
sincere heart.

Scripture Reading

But now in Christ Jesus you
who once were far off have been
brought near by the blood of
Christ. For he is our peace; in his
flesh he has made both groups
into one and has broken down the
dividing wall, that is, the hostility
between us. He has abolished the
law with its commandments and
ordinances, that he might cre-
ate in himself one new humanity
in place of the two, thus mak-
ing peace, and might reconcile
both groups to God in one body
through the cross, thus putting to
death that hostility through it.

(EPHESIANS 2:13–16)

Prayer Response to the Reading

- Listen to us and give us your
 mercy, because we have sinned.

- Christ Jesus, hear our prayer, because we have sinned.
- Glory to the Father, and to the Son, and to the Holy Spirit.
- Listen to us and give us your mercy, because we have sinned.

Gospel Antiphon

Jesus died to bring together all of God's people into one family.

Gospel Canticle

- If you are praying in the morning, pray the morning canticle found on page 249.
- If you are praying in the evening, pray the evening canticle found on page 250.

Glory to the Father, and to the Son, and to the Holy Spirit:
as it was in the beginning, is now, and will be for ever. Amen.

Gospel Antiphon

Jesus died to bring together all of God's people as one family.

Petitions

Jesus, our Savior, has set us free from sin by his sacrifice on the Cross and his Resurrection from the dead. Knowing this love for us, we pray: *Have mercy on us, Lamb of God.*

- Watch over your Church and keep it solid in spite of human weaknesses, we pray. *Have mercy on us, Lamb of God.*
- Help us unite ourselves to you in our suffering and pain, and may we feel your closeness during times of difficulty, we pray. *Have mercy on us, Lamb of God.*
- Bring comfort to those who are homeless, penniless, or under hardships of any kind, we pray. *Have mercy on us, Lamb of God.*
- Teach us to help others, even when we are in the middle of troubles and struggles, we pray. *Have mercy on us, Lamb of God.*
- Lead us to an end of all hostilities and wars against one another, we pray. *Have mercy on us, Lamb of God.*
- At the end of our lives, allow us to be with you forever in Heaven, we pray. *Have mercy on us, Lamb of God.*

Please take time to add your own needs and concerns.

Lord's Prayer

Let us pray in the perfect words
taught to us by Jesus:
Our Father . . .

Closing Prayer

God our Father, the glory of your
Son is revealed to us in the suf-
fering he accepted on our behalf.
Give us the faith we need to
claim as our only goal and need

that same Cross of our Lord Jesus
Christ, your Son, who lives and
reigns with you, in the unity of
the Holy Spirit, one God, forever
and ever. Amen.

Dismissal

May the Lord bless us and pro-
tect us from evil and bring us to
the joy of Heaven. Amen.

Saturday, Week 2

Call to Prayer

God, come to my assistance.
Lord, make haste to help me.
Glory to the Father, and to the
 Son, and to the Holy Spirit:
as it was in the beginning, is now,
 and will be for ever. Amen.

Psalm Antiphon

Blessed are you, Virgin Mary,
because you carried the Creator
of the world in your womb.

Psalm 147:12–20

Praise the LORD, O Jerusalem!
 Praise your God, O Zion!
For he strengthens the bars of
 your gates;
 he blesses your children within
 you.
He grants peace within your
 borders;
 he fills you with the finest of
 wheat.
He sends out his command to
 the earth;
 his word runs swiftly.
He gives snow like wool;
 he scatters frost like ashes.
He hurls down hail like crumbs—
 who can stand before his cold?

He sends out his word, and
 melts them;
 he makes his wind blow, and
 the waters flow.
He declares his word to Jacob,
 his statutes and ordinances
 to Israel.
He has not dealt thus with any
 other nation;
 they do not know his
 ordinances.
Praise the LORD!

Glory to the Father, and to the
 Son, and to the Holy Spirit:
as it was in the beginning, is now,
 and will be for ever. Amen.

Psalm Prayer

You chose to come to us, O
Word of God, through a humble
servant, the Blessed Virgin Mary.
May we also be willing to bring
you into this world by all we say
and do.

Psalm Antiphon

Blessed are you, Virgin Mary,
because you carried the Creator
of the world in your womb.

Scripture Reading

But when the fullness of time had come, God sent his Son, born of a woman, born under the law, in order to redeem those who were under the law, so that we might receive adoption as children.

(GALATIANS 4:4–5)

Prayer Response to the Reading

- The Lord chose her, the one he loved, from the very beginning.
- He has taken her to live with him forever, from the very beginning.
- Glory to the Father, and to the Son, and to the Holy Spirit.
- The Lord chose her, the one he loved, from the very beginning.

Gospel Antiphon

The Lord our God has blessed you, Virgin Mary, above all other women of the world.

Gospel Canticle

- If you are praying in the morning, pray the morning canticle found on page 249.

- If you are praying in the evening, pray the evening canticle found on page 250.

Glory to the Father, and to the Son, and to the Holy Spirit:
as it was in the beginning, is now, and will be for ever. Amen.

Gospel Antiphon

The Lord our God has blessed you, Virgin Mary, above all other women of the world.

Petitions

Let us give thanks to our God, who wished that Mary, the Mother of Jesus, be remembered and honored throughout all time. In need, we pray: *May your Mother intercede for us, O Word of God.*

- You made Mary the Mother of mercy and the Mother of us all. May all who face trouble feel her Motherly love, we pray. *May your Mother intercede for us, O Word of God.*
- You placed Mary as the mother of a family, the home she shared with Joseph and Jesus. Lead all families to reflect this holy model, we

pray. *May your Mother intercede for us, O Word of God.*

- You strengthened Mary as she waited at the foot of the Cross. Give us strength when the struggles of our lives bring us down, we pray. *May your Mother intercede for us, O Word of God.*

- You gave Mary the spiritual ears needed to hear your calling. Help us follow her perfect example of listening to you, we pray. *May your Mother intercede for us, O Word of God.*

- You have set Mary aside for all time as an example of humble service. Lead us to be humble servants to our friends and families, enemies and strangers, we pray. *May your Mother intercede for us, O Word of God.*

- You lifted Mary up to you at the end of her earthly life. May all those who have died rejoice with you and the saints forever, we pray. *May your Mother intercede for us, O Word of God.*

Please take time to add your own needs and concerns.

Lord's Prayer

Let us pray in the perfect words taught to us by Jesus:
Our Father . . .

Closing Prayer

All-powerful Father, in Mary we see what is possible for those who love you with their whole hearts. Through her prayers, help us to be more like her every day, a person who can change the world. We ask this through our Lord, Jesus Christ, your Son, who lives and reigns with you, in the unity of the Holy Spirit, one God, forever and ever. Amen.

Dismissal

May the Lord bless us and protect us from evil and bring us to the joy of Heaven. Amen.

Call to Prayer

God, come to my assistance.
Lord, make haste to help me.
Glory to the Father, and to the
 Son, and to the Holy Spirit:
as it was in the beginning, is now,
 and will be for ever. Amen.

Psalm Antiphon

Praise the name of the Lord.

Psalm 148

Praise the LORD!
Praise the LORD from the heavens;
 praise him in the heights!
Praise him, all his angels;
 praise him, all his host!

Praise him, sun and moon;
 praise him, all you shining stars!
Praise him, you highest heavens,
 and you waters above the
 heavens!

Let them praise the name of
 the LORD,
 for he commanded and they
 were created.
He established them forever
 and ever;
 he fixed their bounds, which
 cannot be passed.

Praise the LORD from the earth,
 you sea monsters and all deeps,
fire and hail, snow and frost,
 stormy wind fulfilling his
 command!

Mountains and all hills,
 fruit trees and all cedars!
Wild animals and all cattle,
 creeping things and flying birds!

Kings of the earth and all peoples,
 princes and all rulers of the
 earth!
Young men and women alike,
 old and young together!

Let them praise the name of
 the LORD,
 for his name alone is exalted;
 his glory is above earth and
 heaven.
He has raised up a horn for his
 people,
 praise for all his faithful,
 for the people of Israel who
 are close to him.
Praise the LORD!

Glory to the Father, and to the
 Son, and to the Holy Spirit:
as it was in the beginning, is now,
 and will be for ever. Amen.

Psalm Prayer

Lord, everything you have created praises you, from the angels in the Heavens above to your children in this world. May heaven and earth join their voices to praise you now and for all eternity.

Psalm Antiphon

Praise the name of the Lord.

Scripture Reading

Blessed be the God and Father of our Lord Jesus Christ! By his great mercy he has given us a new birth into a living hope through the resurrection of Jesus Christ from the dead, and into an inheritance that is imperishable, undefiled, and unfading, kept in heaven for you, who are being protected by the power of God through faith for a salvation ready to be revealed in the last time. In this you rejoice, even if now for a little while you have had to suffer various trials, so that the genuineness of your faith—being more precious than gold that, though perishable, is tested by fire—may be found to result in praise and glory and honor when Jesus Christ is revealed.

(1 PETER 1:3–7)

Prayer Response to the Reading

- All of your creation sings of your greatness and glory.
- Timeless is the praise of your greatness and glory.
- Glory to the Father, and to the Son, and to the Holy Spirit.
- All of your creation sings of your greatness and glory.

Gospel Antiphon

Go and live the Good News: the Reign of God is here!

Gospel Canticle

- If you are praying in the morning, pray the morning canticle found on page 249.
- If you are praying in the evening, pray the evening canticle found on page 250.

Glory to the Father, and to the Son, and to the Holy Spirit: as it was in the beginning, is now, and will be for ever. Amen.

Gospel Antiphon

Go and live the Good News: the Reign of God is here!

Petitions

God continues his creation by renewing the world with his love. In this love, we pray: *Renew your creation, O Source of Life.*

- You gave us the Church as a sign of your love for us. Continue to guide those who lead it and your people, we pray. *Renew your creation, O Source of Life.*

- You gave your Son as the ultimate sacrifice for our sins. May we always do our best to live up to this act of love, we pray. *Renew your creation, O Source of Life.*

- You sent your spirit to Strengthen us to do your work. May we use those gifts to benefit those around us, we pray. *Renew your creation, O Source of Life.*

- You show endless patience with your children. May we learn from your example when dealing with our own families and friends, we pray. *Renew your creation, O Source of Life.*

- You give us what we need to survive. Take special care of those who may go without basic needs this day, we pray. *Renew your creation, O Source of Life.*

- You give us everlasting life with you. Bring into your presence forever those who have gone before us, we pray. *Renew your creation, O Source of Life.*

Please take time to add your own needs and concerns.

Lord's Prayer

Let us pray in the perfect words taught to us by Jesus:
Our Father . . .

Closing Prayer

Almighty God, you are our strength in facing the problems that will come throughout this week. Help us to live a life that reflects our moral convictions and our belief that we are your children, through your Son, Jesus Christ, our Lord, who lives and reigns with you in the unity of the Holy Spirit, one God, forever and ever.

Dismissal

May the Lord bless us and protect us from evil and bring us to the joy of Heaven. Amen.

Monday, Week 3

Call to Prayer

God, come to my assistance.
Lord, make haste to help me.
Glory to the Father, and to the
 Son, and to the Holy Spirit:
as it was in the beginning, is now,
 and will be for ever. Amen.

Psalm Antiphon

Tell the whole world that our
God reigns.

Psalm 96

O sing to the LORD a new song;
 sing to the LORD, all the earth.
Sing to the LORD, bless his name;
 tell of his salvation from day
 to day.
Declare his glory among the
 nations,
 his marvelous works among all
 the peoples.
For great is the LORD, and greatly
 to be praised;
 he is to be revered above all gods.
For all the gods of the peoples
 are idols,
 but the LORD made the heavens.
Honor and majesty are before him;
 strength and beauty are in
 his sanctuary.

Ascribe to the LORD, O families
 of the peoples,
 ascribe to the LORD glory and
 strength.
Ascribe to the LORD the glory
 due his name;
 bring an offering, and come
 into his courts.
Worship the LORD in holy
 splendor;
 tremble before him, all
 the earth.

Say among the nations, "The
 LORD is king!
 The world is firmly established;
 it shall never be moved.
 He will judge the peoples with
 equity."
Let the heavens be glad, and let
 the earth rejoice;
 let the sea roar, and all that
 fills it;
 let the field exult, and
 everything in it.
Then shall all the trees of the
 forest sing for joy
 before the LORD; for he is
 coming,
 for he is coming to judge the
 earth.

He will judge the world with
 righteousness,
 and the peoples with his truth.

Glory to the Father, and to the
 Son, and to the Holy Spirit:
as it was in the beginning, is now,
 and will be for ever. Amen.

Psalm Prayer

Nothing is more worthy of our
celebration than all you have
done for us, Lord. May our praise
of you be another sign of your
love to this world.

Psalm Antiphon

Tell the whole world that our
God reigns.

Scripture Reading

Do not speak evil against one an-
other, brothers and sisters.
 Whoever speaks evil against
another or judges another, speaks
evil against the law and judges
the law; but if you judge the law,
you are not a doer of the law but
a judge. There is one lawgiver and
judge who is able to save and to
destroy. So who, then, are you
to judge your neighbor?

(JAMES 4:11–12)

Prayer Response to the Reading

- Only you can help me, Lord,
 because my sins have hurt you.
- Show me your love and mercy
 because my sins have hurt you.
- Glory to the Father, and to the
 Son, and to the Holy Spirit.
- Only you can help me, Lord,
 because my sins have hurt you.

Gospel Antiphon

Help us in our time of need;
just give the word, and we will
have peace.

Gospel Canticle

- If you are praying in the
 morning, pray the morning
 canticle found on page 249.
- If you are praying in the eve-
 ning, pray the evening canticle
 found on page 250.

Glory to the Father, and to the
 Son, and to the Holy Spirit:
as it was in the beginning, is now,
 and will be for ever. Amen.

Gospel Antiphon

Help us in our time of need;
just give the word and we will
have peace.

Petitions

We give you thanks and praise by the good we do. With hearts full of good intentions, we pray: *Help us do what is good, God of all kindness.*

- Continue to guide leaders around the world to actions that are for the benefit of all people, we pray. *Help us to do what is good, God of all kindness.*

- Give courage to those who lead your pilgrim Church to stand for the Gospel of life, we pray. *Help us to do what is good, God of all kindness.*

- Use us to bring relief to those who are homeless, hungry, and helpless, we pray. *Help us to do what is good, God of all kindness.*

- Enlighten our hearts and minds to see you in those around us who may hurt or anger us, we pray. *Help us to do what is good, God of all kindness.*

- May we see how much you love us through the love of our families and friends, we pray. *Help us to do what is good, God of all kindness.*

- Reward the good of those who have died by granting them

life everlasting with you, we pray. *Help us to do what is good, God of all kindness.*

Please take time to add your own needs and concerns.

Lord's Prayer

Let us pray in the perfect words taught to us by Jesus:
Our Father . . .

Closing Prayer

God, our Father, we need your help in our lives now more than ever. Show us the happiness only you can provide, while we show our thanks to you through our good works. We ask this in the name of Jesus, your Son, and in the power of the Holy Spirit. Amen.

Dismissal

May the Lord bless us and protect us from evil and bring us to the joy of Heaven. Amen.

Tuesday, Week 3

Call to Prayer

God, come to my assistance.
Lord, make haste to help me.
Glory to the Father, and to the
 Son, and to the Holy Spirit:
as it was in the beginning, is now,
 and will be for ever. Amen.

Psalm Antiphon

Shine the light of your love
upon us.

Psalm 67

May God be gracious to us and
 bless us
 and make his face to shine
 upon us,
that your way may be known
 upon earth,
 your saving power among all
 nations.
Let the peoples praise you,
 O God;
 let all the peoples praise you.

Let the nations be glad and sing
 for joy,
 for you judge the peoples with
 equity
 and guide the nations upon
 earth.

Let the peoples praise you,
 O God;
 let all the peoples praise you.

The earth has yielded its increase;
 God, our God, has blessed us.
May God continue to bless us;
 let all the ends of the earth
 revere him.

Glory to the Father, and to the
 Son, and to the Holy Spirit:
as it was in the beginning, is now,
 and will be for ever. Amen.

Psalm Prayer

Bless us, Lord, and shine your love
upon us. Only then can we be
your love in action and serve you.

Psalm Antiphon

Shine the light of your love
upon us.

Scripture Reading

No one has ever seen God; if we
love one another, God lives in us,
and his love is perfected in us.

By this we know that we abide
in him and he in us, because he
has given us of his Spirit. And
we have seen and do testify that

the Father has sent his Son as the Savior of the world. God abides in those who confess that Jesus is the Son of God, and they abide in God.

(1 JOHN 4:12–15)

Prayer Response to the Reading

- I stand with my God, and my God stands with me.
- I spread the Good News of his Son, and he stands with me.
- Glory to the Father, and to the Son, and to the Holy Spirit.
- I stand with my God, and my God stands with me.

Gospel Antiphon

My spirit finds its joy in God.

Gospel Canticle

- If you are praying in the morning, pray the morning canticle found on page 249.
- If you are praying in the evening, pray the evening canticle found on page 250.

Glory to the Father, and to the Son, and to the Holy Spirit: as it was in the beginning, is now, and will be for ever. Amen.

Gospel Antiphon

My spirit finds its joy in God.

Petitions

Because of the love our God has shown us, we are a people filled with hope. It is with this hope that we pray: *Protect your hopeful people, Lord.*

- Protect, Lord, the Holy Father and the bishops, called to lead and serve, we pray. *Protect your hopeful people, Lord.*
- Protect those who have no one to protect them, those who are persecuted, and those who are in pain, we pray. *Protect your hopeful people, Lord.*
- Protect our hearts from the temptations of everyday life that turn our eyes from you, we pray. *Protect your hopeful people, Lord.*
- Protect the work we do and keep it always pleasing to you, we pray. *Protect your hopeful people, Lord.*
- Guard us from words and actions that hurt those around us, we pray. *Protect your hopeful people, Lord.*

- Protect our friends and family members who have gone to their rest by giving them a place with you in Heaven, we pray. *Protect your hopeful people, Lord.*

Please take time to add your own needs and concerns.

Lord's Prayer

Let us pray in the perfect words taught to us by Jesus:
Our Father . . .

Closing Prayer

Merciful God, stay with us, keep us always in your sight, and show us your protective love. Never let us stray from that which makes us truly happy: Jesus Christ, your Son, who lives and reigns with you in the unity of the Holy Spirit, one God, forever and ever. Amen.

Dismissal

May the Lord bless us and protect us from evil and bring us to the joy of Heaven. Amen.

Wednesday, Week 3

Call to Prayer

God, come to my assistance.
Lord, make haste to help me.
Glory to the Father, and to the
 Son, and to the Holy Spirit:
as it was in the beginning, is now,
 and will be for ever. Amen.

Psalm Antiphon

All the world has seen the love
and power of God.

Psalm 98

O sing to the LORD a new song,
 for he has done marvelous
 things.
His right hand and his holy arm
 have gotten him victory.
The LORD has made known his
 victory;
 he has revealed his vindication
 in the sight of the nations.
He has remembered his steadfast
 love and faithfulness
 to the house of Israel.
All the ends of the earth have seen
 the victory of our God.

Make a joyful noise to the LORD,
 all the earth;
 break forth into joyous song
 and sing praises.

Sing praises to the LORD with
 the lyre,
 with the lyre and the sound
 of melody.
With trumpets and the sound
 of the horn
 make a joyful noise before the
 King, the LORD.

Let the sea roar, and all that fills it;
 the world and those who live
 in it.
Let the floods clap their hands;
 let the hills sing together
 for joy
at the presence of the LORD, for
 he is coming
 to judge the earth.
He will judge the world with
 righteousness,
 and the peoples with equity.

Glory to the Father, and to the
 Son, and to the Holy Spirit:
as it was in the beginning, is now,
 and will be for ever. Amen.

Psalm Prayer

Gracious God, fill us up with the
love of your name. Then we will
have the strength to go forth and
bring all people closer to you.

Psalm Antiphon
All the world has seen the love and power of God.

Scripture Reading
I pray that, according to the riches of his glory, he may grant that you may be strengthened in your inner being with power through his Spirit, and that Christ may dwell in your hearts through faith, as you are being rooted and grounded in love. I pray that you may have the power to comprehend, with all the saints, what is the breadth and length and height and depth, and to know the love of Christ that surpasses knowledge, so that you may be filled with all the fullness of God.

Now to him who by the power at work within us is able to accomplish abundantly far more than all we can ask or imagine, to him be glory in the church and in Christ Jesus to all generations, forever and ever. Amen.

(EPHESIANS 3:16–21)

Prayer Response to the Reading
- Claim us as your own and show us mercy.

- Do not leave us to fend for ourselves, and show us mercy.
- Glory to the Father, and to the Son, and to the Holy Spirit.
- Claim us as your own and show us mercy.

Gospel Antiphon
Show us mercy, Lord, and remember the covenant you have made with us.

Gospel Canticle
- If you are praying in the morning, pray the morning canticle found on page 249.
- If you are praying in the evening, pray the evening canticle found on page 250.

Glory to the Father, and to the Son, and to the Holy Spirit:
as it was in the beginning, is now, and will be for ever. Amen.

Gospel Antiphon
Show us mercy, Lord, and remember the covenant you have made with us.

Petitions
What God can do for us and through us is more than we could

ever imagine. Keeping this in mind, we pray: *Gentle Master, help us to help one another.*

- Help those who lead your Church to be faithful to you in word and in deed, we pray. *Gentle Master, help us to help one another.*

- Help those who do not know the power of your love and are searching for the truth, we pray. *Gentle Master, help us to help one another.*

- Help those who are most helpless in this world: children, both born and unborn, the elderly, the sick, and the suffering, we pray. *Gentle Master, help us to help one another.*

- Help us always to look for your hand in the good things around us and to be thankful for your blessings, we pray. *Gentle Master, help us to help one another.*

- Help us forgive those who have hurt us, misused our trust, or taken us for granted, we pray. *Gentle Master, help us to help one another.*

- Help prepare our souls for a place at the heavenly table with those who have gone before us, we pray. *Gentle Master, help us to help one another.*

Please take time to add your own needs and concerns.

Lord's Prayer

Let us pray in the perfect words taught to us by Jesus:
Our Father . . .

Closing Prayer

God of mercy and hope, your love for your children is greater than our hearts and minds could know and hold. Help us to see and feel that love and spread it to our friends, families, and all those around us, so that all may know the happiness you bring. We ask this through our Lord, Jesus Christ, your Son, who lives and reigns with you in the unity of the Holy Spirit, one God, forever and ever. Amen.

Dismissal

May the Lord bless us and protect us from evil and bring us to the joy of Heaven. Amen.

Thursday, Week 3

Call to Prayer

God, come to my assistance.
Lord, make haste to help me.
Glory to the Father, and to the
 Son, and to the Holy Spirit:
as it was in the beginning, is now,
 and will be for ever. Amen.

Psalm Antiphon

Come quickly and help
your people.

Psalm 99

The LORD is king; let the peoples
 tremble!
 He sits enthroned upon the
 cherubim; let the earth
 quake!
The LORD is great in Zion;
 he is exalted over all the
 peoples.
Let them praise your great and
 awesome name.
 Holy is he!
Mighty King, lover of justice,
 you have established equity;
you have executed justice
 and righteousness in Jacob.
Extol the LORD our God;
 worship at his footstool.
 Holy is he!

Moses and Aaron were among
 his priests,
 Samuel also was among those
 who called on his name.
 They cried to the LORD, and
 he answered them.
He spoke to them in the pillar
 of cloud;
 they kept his decrees,
 and the statutes that he gave
 them.

O LORD our God, you answered
 them;
 you were a forgiving God to
 them,
 but an avenger of their
 wrongdoings.
Extol the LORD our God,
 and worship at his holy
 mountain;
 for the LORD our God is holy.

Glory to the Father, and to the
 Son, and to the Holy Spirit:
as it was in the beginning, is now,
 and will be for ever. Amen.

Psalm Prayer

You have power over all your
people, mighty God, but you
gently answer those who call out
to you in faith. Bless us, your

people, and continue to give us what we truly need.

Psalm Antiphon

Come quickly and help your people.

Scripture Reading

Finally, all of you, have unity of spirit, sympathy, love for one another, a tender heart, and a humble mind. Do not repay evil for evil or abuse for abuse; but, on the contrary, repay with a blessing. It is for this that you were called—that you might inherit a blessing. For

> "Those who desire life and
> desire to see good days,
> let them keep their tongues
> from evil
> and their lips from
> speaking deceit;
> let them turn away from evil
> and do good;
> let them seek peace and
> pursue it.
> For the eyes of the Lord are on
> the righteous,
> and his ears are open to
> their prayer.
> But the face of the Lord is
> against those who do evil."

(1 PETER 3:8–12)

Prayer Response to the Reading

- You satisfy our hungers with bread made of the finest wheat.
- Give us in your mercy, loving God, bread made of the finest wheat.
- Glory to the Father, and to the Son, and to the Holy Spirit.
- You satisfy our hungers with bread made of the finest wheat.

Gospel Antiphon

I am the living bread from Heaven. Eat this bread, and you will live forever.

Gospel Canticle

- If you are praying in the morning, pray the morning canticle found on page 249.
- If you are praying in the evening, pray the evening canticle found on page 250.

Glory to the Father, and to the Son, and to the Holy Spirit:
as it was in the beginning, is now, and will be for ever. Amen.

Gospel Antiphon

I am the living bread from Heaven. Eat this bread, and you will live forever.

Petitions

Let us call out to God, our Father in Heaven, who feeds his people and watches us with love. With humility, we pray: *Hear your people who hunger.*

- Give faith, hope, and charity to the Pope and all bishops and help them to be models of service, we pray. *Hear your people who hunger.*

- Give those who are open to being converted to the Gospel the will to succeed and the strength from your Holy Spirit to fight on, we pray. *Hear your people who hunger.*

- Give peace of mind and heart to those who are far from the safety of home and family, we pray. *Hear your people who hunger.*

- Give those who want to serve you with good intentions the guidance and wisdom never to wander from your gaze, we pray. *Hear your people who hunger.*

- Give us patience when dealing with our friends and family members who upset us or cause us grief, we pray. *Hear your people who hunger.*

- Give our departed brothers and sisters a place with you in Heaven, we pray. *Hear your people who hunger.*

Please take time to add your own needs and concerns.

Lord's Prayer

Let us pray in the perfect words taught to us by Jesus:
Our Father . . .

Closing Prayer

Father, hear the prayer we give you as a gift. In return, feed our hearts and minds with your gifts, so we can live as you want us to live: a people filled with hope and wanting only to serve you. We ask this in the name of Jesus, the Lord, in the power of the Holy Spirit. Amen.

Dismissal

May the Lord bless us and protect us from evil and bring us to the joy of Heaven. Amen.

Friday, Week 3

Call to Prayer

God, come to my assistance.
Lord, make haste to help me.
Glory to the Father, and to the
 Son, and to the Holy Spirit:
as it was in the beginning, is now,
 and will be for ever. Amen.

Psalm Antiphon

Wash me of my sins, Lord.

Psalm 51

Have mercy on me, O God,
 according to your steadfast
 love;
according to your abundant mercy
 blot out my transgressions.
Wash me thoroughly from my
 iniquity,
 and cleanse me from my sin.

For I know my transgressions,
 and my sin is ever before me.
Against you, you alone, have
 I sinned,
 and done what is evil in your
 sight,
so that you are justified in your
 sentence
 and blameless when you pass
 judgment.

Indeed, I was born guilty,
 a sinner when my mother
 conceived me.

You desire truth in the inward
 being;
 therefore teach me wisdom in
 my secret heart.
Purge me with hyssop, and I shall
 be clean;
 wash me, and I shall be whiter
 than snow.
Let me hear joy and gladness;
 let the bones that you have
 crushed rejoice.
Hide your face from my sins,
 and blot out all my iniquities.

Create in me a clean heart, O God,
 and put a new and right spirit
 within me.
Do not cast me away from your
 presence,
 and do not take your holy
 spirit from me.
Restore to me the joy of your
 salvation,
 and sustain in me a willing
 spirit.

Then I will teach transgressors
 your ways,
 and sinners will return to you.

Deliver me from bloodshed,
 O God,
 O God of my salvation,
 and my tongue will sing aloud
 of your deliverance.

O Lord, open my lips,
 and my mouth will declare
 your praise.
For you have no delight in sacrifice;
 if I were to give a burnt
 offering, you would not
 be pleased.
The sacrifice acceptable to God is
 a broken spirit;
 a broken and contrite heart, O
 God, you will not despise.

Do good to Zion in your good
 pleasure;
 rebuild the walls of Jerusalem,
then you will delight in right
 sacrifices,
 in burnt offerings and whole
 burnt offerings;
 then bulls will be offered on
 your altar.

Glory to the Father, and to the
 Son, and to the Holy Spirit:
as it was in the beginning, is now,
 and will be for ever. Amen.

Psalm Prayer

Father, you sent your only Son, perfect and without sin, into this world to forgive the sins of your people. May we continue to do all we can in our lives to live up to that incredible gift.

Psalm Antiphon

Wash me of my sins, Lord.

Scripture Reading

My brothers and sisters, whenever you face trials of any kind, consider it nothing but joy, because you know that the testing of your faith produces endurance; and let endurance have its full effect, so that you may be mature and complete, lacking in nothing.

If any of you is lacking in wisdom, ask God, who gives to all generously and ungrudgingly, and it will be given you. But ask in faith, never doubting, for the one who doubts is like a wave of the sea, driven and tossed by the wind; for the doubter, being double-minded and unstable in every way, must not expect to receive anything from the Lord.

(JAMES 1:2–8)

Prayer Response to the Reading

- Christ loves us always and frees us from our sin.
- He feeds us with his Body and Blood, and frees us from our sin.
- Glory to the Father, and to the Son, and to the Holy Spirit.
- Christ loves us always and frees us from our sin.

Gospel Antiphon

What good does it do if you gain all the riches of the world and pay for it with your soul?

Gospel Canticle

- If you are praying in the morning, pray the morning canticle found on page 249.
- If you are praying in the evening, pray the evening canticle found on page 250.

Glory to the Father, and to the Son, and to the Holy Spirit:

as it was in the beginning, is now, and will be for ever. Amen.

Gospel Antiphon

What good does it do if you gain all the riches of the world and pay for it with your soul?

Petitions

We keep our eyes on Christ, our Lord, who came into this world, died, and rose again for us. With this perfect example in our sight, we pray: *Save your people, God of victory.*

- See the good your daughters and sons do for the benefit of others and give them what they need to continue, we pray. *Save your people, God of victory.*
- Continue to call forth leaders and servants for your Church, and give them the courage to answer, we pray. *Save your people, God of victory.*
- Protect us from ourselves, from the actions we do in our daily lives that take us from you, we pray. *Save your people, God of victory.*
- Let us be an example of your love and care to those around us: family, friends, and strangers, we pray. *Save your people, God of victory.*
- Look on the suffering of those in this world who are hurting and suffering through no fault of their own and bless them for it, we pray. *Save your people, God of victory.*

- Lead all souls to Heaven, especially those who need your mercy the most, we pray. *Save your people, God of victory.*

Please take time to add your own needs and concerns.

Lord's Prayer

Let us pray in the perfect words taught to us by Jesus:
Our Father . . .

Closing Prayer

Father, you sent Jesus to save your adopted children from themselves. Help us to change our lives from something burdened by sin to a sign of your glory and love for all we see. We ask this through the same Jesus Christ, our Lord, and in the power of the Holy Spirit. Amen.

Dismissal

May the Lord bless us and protect us from evil and bring us to the joy of Heaven. Amen.

Saturday, Week 3

Call to Prayer

God, come to my assistance.
Lord, make haste to help me.
Glory to the Father, and to the
 Son, and to the Holy Spirit:
as it was in the beginning, is now,
 and will be for ever. Amen.

Psalm Antiphon

Blessed are you, Virgin Mary,
because you carried the Creator
of the world in your womb.

Psalm 122

I was glad when they said to me,
 "Let us go to the house of
 the Lord!"
Our feet are standing
 within your gates, O Jerusalem.

Jerusalem—built as a city
 that is bound firmly together.
To it the tribes go up,
 the tribes of the Lord,
as was decreed for Israel,
 to give thanks to the name
 of the Lord.
For there the thrones for
 judgment were set up,
 the thrones of the house of
 David.

Pray for the peace of Jerusalem:
 "May they prosper who love
 you.
Peace be within your walls,
 and security within your
 towers."
For the sake of my relatives and
 friends
 I will say, "Peace be within you."
For the sake of the house of the
 Lord our God,
 I will seek your good.

Glory to the Father, and to the
 Son, and to the Holy Spirit:
as it was in the beginning, is now,
 and will be for ever. Amen.

Psalm Prayer

The Blessed Virgin Mary did
what you asked her to do,
Lord, and never faltered. For
the sake of your Kingdom,
for the sake of our friends and
families, and for the sake of our
own salvation, may we follow her
perfect example.

Psalm Antiphon

Blessed are you, Virgin Mary,
because you carried the Creator
of the world in your womb.

Scripture Reading

A great portent appeared in heaven:
a woman clothed with the sun, with
the moon under her feet, and on
her head a crown of twelve stars.

(REVELATION 12:1)

Prayer Response
to the Reading

- Holy Mary, mother of God,
 pray for us sinners.
- Now and at the hour of our
 death pray for us sinners.
- Glory to the Father, and to the
 Son, and to the Holy Spirit.
- Holy Mary, mother of God,
 pray for us sinners.

Gospel Antiphon

You received a child from
Heaven, and you gave birth to
the Savior of the world.

Gospel Canticle

- If you are praying in the
 morning, pray the morning
 canticle found on page 249.
- If you are praying in the eve-
 ning, pray the evening canticle
 found on page 250.

Glory to the Father, and to the
 Son, and to the Holy Spirit:
as it was in the beginning, is now,
 and will be for ever. Amen.

Gospel Antiphon

You received a child from
Heaven, and you gave birth to
the Savior of the world.

Petitions

Celebrate Jesus Christ, our Lord,
who is the Son of God and the
son of Mary. With confidence,
we pray: *May your Mother inter-
cede for us, our Savior.*

- You gave Mary a share in your
 saving mission. Strengthen all
 those who share in this mission
 today, we pray. *May your Mother
 intercede for us, our Savior.*
- You blessed Mary with the
 grace to accept all the trials
 and struggles that came with
 her calling. Give us the same
 grace to overcome those trials
 in our daily lives, we pray.
 *May your Mother intercede for
 us, our Savior.*
- You lived in this world with
 Mary and Joseph in a holy
 family. Help our own families

model this beautiful example, we pray. *May your Mother intercede for us, our Savior.*

- The servants at the wedding feast followed your words only after your Mother told them they should. Open our ears to your words with the help of Mary, we pray. *May your Mother intercede for us, our Savior.*

- Your Mother witnessed your pain and suffering at the hands of others and never struck back. Help us to endure those who hurt us with the same resolve your Mother had, we pray. *May your Mother intercede for us, our Savior.*

- Mary's reward for her faithfulness and love was a place with you in Heaven. Grant this same gift to those who have died, we pray. *May your Mother intercede for us, our Savior.*

Please take time to add your own needs and concerns.

Lord's Prayer

Let us pray in the perfect words taught to us by Jesus:
Our Father . . .

Closing Prayer

God, our Father, you set Mary apart from the beginning of time as an example of what we can be if we have faith in your words. Listen to her prayers on our behalf and give us what we need to be faithful and holy as she is faithful and holy. We ask this through our Lord, Jesus Christ, your Son, who lives and reigns with you in the unity of the Holy Spirit, one God, forever and ever. Amen.

Dismissal

May the Lord bless us and protect us from evil and bring us to the joy of Heaven. Amen.

Sunday, Week 4

Call to Prayer

God, come to my assistance.
Lord, make haste to help me.
Glory to the Father, and to the
 Son, and to the Holy Spirit:
as it was in the beginning, is now,
 and will be for ever. Amen.

Psalm Antiphon

Praise the Lord, for all that he
does is perfect and right.

Psalm 150

Praise the LORD!
Praise God in his sanctuary;
 praise him in his mighty
 firmament!
Praise him for his mighty deeds;
 praise him according to his
 surpassing greatness!

Praise him with trumpet sound;
 praise him with lute and harp!
Praise him with tambourine
 and dance;
 praise him with strings and pipe!
Praise him with clanging cymbals;
 praise him with loud clashing
 cymbals!
Let everything that breathes
 praise the LORD!
Praise the LORD!

Glory to the Father, and to the
 Son, and to the Holy Spirit:
as it was in the beginning, is now,
 and will be for ever. Amen.

Psalm Prayer

Hear the songs of thanks your
people sing to you, Holy God,
and give them what they need
to do the work of the Gospel in
their lives.

Psalm Antiphon

Praise the Lord, for all that he
does is perfect and right.

Scripture Reading

Remember Jesus Christ, raised
from the dead, a descendant of
David—that is my gospel. . . .
The saying is sure:
 If we have died with him, we
 will also live with him;
 if we endure, we will also reign
 with him;
 if we deny him, he will also
 deny us;
 if we are faithless, he remains
 faithful—
 for he cannot deny himself.

(2 TIMOTHY 2:8,11–13)

Prayer Response to the Reading

- We thank you for your love and faithfulness to us.
- Singing songs of praise and worship for your love and faithfulness to us.
- Glory to the Father, and to the Son, and to the Holy Spirit.
- We thank you for your love and faithfulness to us.

Gospel Antiphon

The name of the Lord is praised both on earth and in the heavens.

Gospel Canticle

- If you are praying in the morning, pray the morning canticle found on page 249.
- If you are praying in the evening, pray the evening canticle found on page 250.

Glory to the Father, and to the Son, and to the Holy Spirit:
as it was in the beginning, is now, and will be for ever. Amen.

Gospel Antiphon

The name of the Lord is praised both on earth and in the heavens.

Petitions

Our spirit finds joy and peace in our God, who gives us all good things. With happiness, we pray: *Be our life, O source of life.*

- Give those who lead your Church what they need to be faithful and true to the Gospel, we pray. *Be our life, O source of life.*
- Give food and drink, shelter and clothing, and the peace of your love to those who go without these essentials for human dignity, we pray. *Be our life, O source of life.*
- Give us patience and understanding as we strive to do what is right in dealing with our friends and family, we pray. *Be our life, O source of life.*
- Give all those who seek your ways courage to answer your call, we pray. *Be our life, O source of life.*
- Give hope to all those who cannot feel your presence in their lives, we pray. *Be our life, O Source of Life.*
- Give the gift of eternal life to those who have gone before

us, we pray. *Be our life, O source of life.*

Please take time to add your own needs and concerns.

Lord's Prayer

Let us pray in the perfect words taught to us by Jesus:
Our Father . . .

Closing Prayer

Almighty God, help us to proclaim your saving power in all we say and do. Enlighten our minds and enkindle our hearts to think and love more like Jesus, your Son, who lives and reigns with you in the unity of the Holy Spirit, one God, forever and ever. Amen.

Dismissal

May the Lord bless us and protect us from evil and bring us to the joy of Heaven. Amen.

Monday, Week 4

Call to Prayer

God, come to my assistance.
Lord, make haste to help me.
Glory to the Father, and to the
 Son, and to the Holy Spirit:
as it was in the beginning, is now,
 and will be for ever. Amen.

Psalm Antiphon

The God of Light has called
you out of the darkness into the
splendor of light.

Psalm 136:1–9

O give thanks to the LORD, for
 he is good,
 for his steadfast love endures
 forever.
O give thanks to the God of gods,
 for his steadfast love endures
 forever.
O give thanks to the Lord of lords,
 for his steadfast love endures
 forever;

who alone does great wonders,
 for his steadfast love endures
 forever;
who by understanding made the
 heavens,
 for his steadfast love endures
 forever;

who spread out the earth on
 the waters,
 for his steadfast love endures
 forever;
who made the great lights,
 for his steadfast love endures
 forever;
the sun to rule over the day,
 for his steadfast love endures
 forever;
the moon and stars to rule over
 the night,
 for his steadfast love endures
 forever.

Glory to the Father, and to the
 Son, and to the Holy Spirit:
as it was in the beginning, is now,
 and will be for ever. Amen.

Psalm Prayer

Father, our lives are constantly
changing. But your love for us
lasts forever. Hear our prayer
of praise and grant that we will
never turn our backs on your
steadfast love.

Psalm Antiphon

The God of Light has called
you out of the darkness into the
splendor of light.

Scripture Reading

And may the Lord make you increase and abound in love for one another and for all, just as we abound in love for you. And may he so strengthen your hearts in holiness that you may be blameless before our God and Father at the coming of our Lord Jesus with all his saints.

(1 Thessalonians 3:12–13)

Prayer Response to the Reading

- Give thanks to the Lord, for his is a love without end.
- He shows us mercy and compassion, for his is a love without end.
- Glory to the Father, and to the Son, and to the Holy Spirit.
- Give thanks to the Lord, for his is a love without end.

Gospel Antiphon

Bless the Lord, who has come to his people and set them free.

Gospel Canticle

- If you are praying in the morning, pray the morning canticle found on page 249.

- If you are praying in the evening, pray the evening canticle found on page 250.

Glory to the Father, and to the
 Son, and to the Holy Spirit:
as it was in the beginning, is now,
 and will be for ever. Amen.

Gospel Antiphon

Bless the Lord, who has come to his people and set them free.

Petitions

Because God has proven to be always faithful, we have hope for a future in God's love. Mindful of this, we pray: *Answer your hopeful people.*

- Eternal High Priest, strengthen those who serve the members of your Church on earth, we pray. *Answer your hopeful people.*
- Light to the nations, guide the actions of world leaders and help them to do your will, we pray. *Answer your hopeful people.*
- Son of David, bring healing to those who are sick and suffering, we pray. *Answer your hopeful people.*

- Son of Mary, show us how to follow you in faith and trust, we pray. *Answer your hopeful people.*
- Servant of all, help us to be like you in our relationships with family and friends—supportive, patient, and forgiving, we pray. *Answer your hopeful people.*
- Risen Lord, grant eternal life to all those who have served you in love and have gone on to their reward, we pray. *Answer your hopeful people.*

Please take time to add your own needs and concerns.

Lord's Prayer

Let us pray in the perfect words taught to us by Jesus:
Our Father . . .

Closing Prayer

Father, you are our constant companion, always there to guide our ways. Help us to recognize that you are with us in Scripture and in the breaking of the bread. We ask this in the name of Jesus, your Son, and in the power of the Holy Spirit. Amen.

Dismissal

May the Lord bless us and protect us from evil and bring us to the joy of Heaven. Amen.

Tuesday, Week 4

Call to Prayer

God, come to my assistance.
Lord, make haste to help me.
Glory to the Father, and to the
 Son, and to the Holy Spirit:
as it was in the beginning, is now,
 and will be for ever. Amen.

Psalm Antiphon

I can do all things in the name of
the one who has given me power.

Psalm 144:1–10

Blessed be the LORD, my rock,
 who trains my hands for war,
 and my fingers for battle;
my rock and my fortress,
 my stronghold and my
 deliverer,
my shield, in whom I take refuge,
 who subdues the peoples under
 me.

O LORD, what are human beings
 that you regard them,
 or mortals that you think of
 them?
They are like a breath;
 their days are like a passing
 shadow.

Bow your heavens, O LORD, and
 come down;

touch the mountains so that
 they smoke.
Make the lightning flash and
 scatter them;
 send out your arrows and rout
 them.
Stretch out your hand from on high;
 set me free and rescue me
 from the mighty waters,
 from the hand of aliens,
whose mouths speak lies,
 and whose right hands are
 false.

I will sing a new song to you,
 O God;
 upon a ten-stringed harp I will
 play to you,
the one who gives victory to kings,
 who rescues his servant David.

Glory to the Father, and to the
 Son, and to the Holy Spirit:
as it was in the beginning, is now,
 and will be for ever. Amen.

Psalm Prayer

God of power and might, you
give us the gifts to fight the evil
we encounter. Watch over and
protect your people, keeping
them safe from harm and ready
to do your will.

Psalm Antiphon

I can do all things in the name of the one who has given me power.

Scripture Reading

And let the peace of Christ rule in your hearts, to which indeed you were called in the one body. And be thankful. Let the word of Christ dwell in you richly; teach and admonish one another in all wisdom; and with gratitude in your hearts sing psalms, hymns, and spiritual songs to God. And whatever you do, in word or deed, do everything in the name of the Lord Jesus, giving thanks to God the Father through him.

(Colossians 3:15–17)

Prayer Response to the Reading

- Turn to the Lord, your God, with your whole heart, and he will cleanse you of your sins.
- Show a heart that is humble and repentant, and he will cleanse you of your sins.
- Glory to the Father, and to the Son, and to the Holy Spirit.
- Turn to the Lord, your God, with your whole heart, and God will cleanse you of your sins.

Gospel Antiphon

God comes from Heaven above to save his people.

Gospel Canticle

- If you are praying in the morning, pray the morning canticle found on page 249.
- If you are praying in the evening, pray the evening canticle found on page 250.

Glory to the Father, and to the Son, and to the Holy Spirit:
as it was in the beginning, is now, and will be for ever. Amen.

Gospel Antiphon

God comes from Heaven above to save his people.

Petitions

We thank Christ, our Lord, who gives the people of God strength and power to journey toward Heaven. With confidence, we pray: *Protect your pilgrim people, Christ, our shepherd.*

- Continue to send courageous leaders to your Church on earth, ministers to lead and serve your children, we pray. *Protect your pilgrim people, Christ, our shepherd.*

- Bless and protect those who are most in need, the unborn, the sick, and those who have no one to stand up for them, we pray. *Protect your pilgrim people, Christ, our shepherd.*

- Keep us safe and free from the temptations in our daily lives that lead us from your love, we pray. *Protect your pilgrim people, Christ, our shepherd.*

- See our love for you in the good we try to do and forgive us for those times we may hurt others or ourselves, we pray. *Protect your pilgrim people, Christ, our shepherd.*

- Take special care of those around us, our family, friends, and strangers, who make your love present to us in what they say and do, we pray. *Protect your pilgrim people, Christ, our shepherd.*

- Reward with eternal life those who have completed their earthly pilgrimages, we pray. *Protect your pilgrim people, Christ, our shepherd.*

Please take time to add your own needs and concerns.

Lord's Prayer

Let us pray in the perfect words taught to us by Jesus:
Our Father . . .

Closing Prayer

God, our Father, you sent your Son to us as the ideal we all long to be. In him, you have adopted us as your own sons and daughters. Help the words we say and the actions we take match the love we hold in our hearts. We ask this in the name of Jesus, the Lord, in the unity of the Holy Spirit. Amen.

Dismissal

May the Lord bless us and protect us from evil and bring us to the joy of Heaven. Amen.

Wednesday, Week 4

Call to Prayer

God, come to my assistance.
Lord, make haste to help me.
Glory to the Father, and to the
 Son, and to the Holy Spirit:
as it was in the beginning, is now,
 and will be for ever. Amen.

Psalm Antiphon

Those who put their trust in God
know what true happiness is.

Psalm 146

Praise the LORD!
Praise the LORD, O my soul!
I will praise the LORD as long as
 I live;
 I will sing praises to my God
 all my life long.

Do not put your trust in princes,
 in mortals, in whom there is
 no help.
When their breath departs, they
 return to the earth;
 on that very day their plans
 perish.

Happy are those whose help is
 the God of Jacob,
 whose hope is in the LORD
 their God,

who made heaven and earth,
 the sea, and all that is in them;
who keeps faith forever;
 who executes justice for the
 oppressed;
 who gives food to the hungry.

The LORD sets the prisoners free;
 the LORD opens the eyes of
 the blind.
The LORD lifts up those who are
 bowed down;
 the LORD loves the righteous.
The LORD watches over the
 strangers;
 he upholds the orphan and
 the widow,
 but the way of the wicked he
 brings to ruin.

The LORD will reign forever,
 your God, O Zion, for all
 generations.
Praise the LORD!

Glory to the Father, and to the
 Son, and to the Holy Spirit:
as it was in the beginning, is now,
 and will be for ever. Amen.

Psalm Prayer

The only way to find the happiness we long for is to place our

trust in you, Lord. Keep our eyes always fixed on you and our hearts open to your love.

Psalm Antiphon

Those who put their trust in God know what true happiness is.

Scripture Reading

Now by this we may be sure that we know him, if we obey his commandments. Whoever says, "I have come to know him," but does not obey his commandments, is a liar, and in such a person the truth does not exist; but whoever obeys his word, truly in this person the love of God has reached perfection. By this we may be sure that we are in him: whoever says, "I abide in him," ought to walk just as he walked.

(1 JOHN 2:3–6)

Prayer Response to the Reading

- My heart is ready, O God, my heart is ready.
- Because I have come to know you and listen to your words, my heart is ready.
- Glory to the Father, and to the Son, and to the Holy Spirit.

- My heart is ready, O God, my heart is ready.

Gospel Antiphon

Lord, I love to listen to your word.

Gospel Canticle

- If you are praying in the morning, pray the morning canticle found on page 249.
- If you are praying in the evening, pray the evening canticle found on page 250.

Glory to the Father, and to the Son, and to the Holy Spirit:
as it was in the beginning, is now, and will be for ever. Amen.

Gospel Antiphon

Lord, I love to listen to your word.

Petitions

Jesus is the Word of God, and his message is Good News for all people. Thankful for this gift, we pray: Hear us, Word of God.

- Watch over those who shepherd the Church, our Holy Father and the bishops, the descendants of the Apostles, and keep them true to the Gospel, we pray. *Hear us, Word of God.*

- Make us mindful of our own words, words that can hurt or words that can heal, and guide our thoughts and speech, we pray. *Hear us, Word of God.*

- Your Word brings peace to those who hear it. Send it to those places of violence and unrest that need it the most, we pray. *Hear us, Word of God.*

- With only a word, you healed the sick among you. Bring comfort and relief to those in our lives who are ailing in body or spirit, we pray. *Hear us, Word of God.*

- You forgave those who tried to harm you with words of hate. Give us the wisdom to forgive others as you did, we pray. *Hear us, Word of God.*

- You have the words of everlasting life. Grant this to our brothers and sisters who have died, we pray. *Hear us, Word of God.*

Please take time to add your own needs and concerns.

Lord's Prayer

Let us pray in the perfect words taught to us by Jesus:
Our Father . . .

Closing Prayer

God, you raised up a fallen world by sending your Son as our redeemer. Open our hearts to his words and forgive us when we do not listen. We ask this in the name of our Lord, Jesus Christ, your Son, who lives and reigns with you in the unity of the Holy Spirit, one God, forever and ever. Amen.

Dismissal

May the Lord bless us and protect us from evil and bring us to the joy of Heaven. Amen.

Thursday, Week 4

Call to Prayer

God, come to my assistance.
Lord, make haste to help me.
Glory to the Father, and to the
 Son, and to the Holy Spirit:
as it was in the beginning, is now,
 and will be for ever. Amen.

Psalm Antiphon

The Lord rebuilds Jerusalem and
heals the brokenhearted.

Psalm 147:1–11

Praise the LORD!
How good it is to sing praises to
 our God;
 for he is gracious, and a song
 of praise is fitting.
The LORD builds up Jerusalem;
 he gathers the outcasts of
 Israel.
He heals the brokenhearted,
 and binds up their wounds.
He determines the number of
 the stars;
 he gives to all of them their
 names.
Great is our Lord, and abundant
 in power;
 his understanding is beyond
 measure.

The LORD lifts up the
 downtrodden;
 he casts the wicked to the
 ground.

Sing to the LORD with
 thanksgiving;
 make melody to our God on
 the lyre.
He covers the heavens with
 clouds,
 prepares rain for the earth,
 makes grass grow on the hills.
He gives to the animals their
 food,
 and to the young ravens when
 they cry.
His delight is not in the strength
 of the horse,
 nor his pleasure in the speed
 of a runner;
but the LORD takes pleasure in
 those who fear him,
 in those who hope in his
 steadfast love.

Glory to the Father, and to the
 Son, and to the Holy Spirit:
as it was in the beginning, is now,
 and will be for ever. Amen.

Psalm Prayer

God, our Father, you know the number of the stars in the sky, because your life-giving hand placed them there. Heal our broken hearts, gather us into one people, and bless us with your wisdom and grace.

Psalm Antiphon

The Lord rebuilds Jerusalem and heals the brokenhearted.

Scripture Reading

I consider that the sufferings of this present time are not worth comparing with the glory about to be revealed to us. For the creation waits with eager longing for the revealing of the children of God; for the creation was subjected to futility, not of its own will but by the will of the one who subjected it, in hope that the creation itself will be set free from its bondage to decay and will obtain the freedom of the glory of the children of God.

(ROMANS 8:18–21)

Prayer Response to the Reading

- Blessed are the people who have put their faith in God, the Savior.
- The sufferings of the present time will be nothing to the people who have put their faith in God, the Savior.
- Glory to the Father, and to the Son, and to the Holy Spirit.
- Blessed are the people who have put their faith in God, the Savior.

Gospel Antiphon

I am the way, the truth, and the life; no one comes to the Father unless it is through me.

Gospel Canticle

- If you are praying in the morning, pray the morning canticle found on page 249.
- If you are praying in the evening, pray the evening canticle found on page 250.

Glory to the Father, and to the Son, and to the Holy Spirit: as it was in the beginning, is now, and will be for ever. Amen.

Gospel Antiphon

I am the way, the truth, and the life; no one comes to the Father unless it is through me.

Petitions

We pray to Christ, the light of the world and the joy of all creation, as we say: *Lead us to glory by your light.*

- Watch over your Church and help those who are called to lead it to be faithful and joy-filled people, we pray. *Lead us to glory by your light.*

- Shine your light over all the earth, so that every person may hear your name and know the wonders of your love, we pray. *Lead us to glory by your light.*

- Bring us out of the darkness brought on by our own sin and weakness, we pray. *Lead us to glory by your light.*

- Make us an example of your glory to all we encounter, family and friends, strangers and enemies, we pray. *Lead us to glory by your light.*

- Take care of those who are homeless, penniless, and in need of the joy of your presence, we pray. *Lead us to glory by your light.*

- Grant eternal rest to our departed brothers and sisters, and may your perpetual light shine upon them, we pray. *Lead us to glory by your light.*

Please take time to add your own needs and concerns.

Lord's Prayer

Let us pray in the perfect words taught to us by Jesus:
Our Father . . .

Closing Prayer

Father, let the knowledge of your love enlighten our hearts and minds and allow us to serve you fearlessly and freely, giving you the glory that is due. We ask this through our Lord, Jesus Christ, your Son, who lives and reigns with you in the unity of the Holy Spirit, one God, forever and ever. Amen.

Dismissal

May the Lord bless us and protect us from evil and bring us to the joy of Heaven. Amen.

Friday, Week 4

Call to Prayer

God, come to my assistance.
Lord, make haste to help me.
Glory to the Father, and to the
 Son, and to the Holy Spirit:
as it was in the beginning, is now,
 and will be for ever. Amen.

Psalm Antiphon

Deliver me from bloodshed, God
of my salvation.

Psalm 51

Have mercy on me, O God,
 according to your steadfast love;
according to your abundant mercy
 blot out my transgressions.
Wash me thoroughly from my
 iniquity,
 and cleanse me from my sin.

For I know my transgressions,
 and my sin is ever before me.
Against you, you alone, have I
 sinned,
 and done what is evil in your
 sight,
so that you are justified in your
 sentence
 and blameless when you pass
 judgment.

Indeed, I was born guilty,
 a sinner when my mother
 conceived me.

You desire truth in the inward
 being;
 therefore teach me wisdom in
 my secret heart.
Purge me with hyssop, and I shall
 be clean;
 wash me, and I shall be whiter
 than snow.
Let me hear joy and gladness;
 let the bones that you have
 crushed rejoice.
Hide your face from my sins,
 and blot out all my iniquities.

Create in me a clean heart, O God,
 and put a new and right spirit
 within me.
Do not cast me away from your
 presence,
 and do not take your holy
 spirit from me.
Restore to me the joy of your
 salvation,
 and sustain in me a willing
 spirit.

Then I will teach transgressors
 your ways,
 and sinners will return to you.

Deliver me from bloodshed,
 O God,
 O God of my salvation,
 and my tongue will sing aloud
 of your deliverance.

O Lord, open my lips,
 and my mouth will declare
 your praise.
For you have no delight in
 sacrifice;
 if I were to give a burnt
 offering, you would not
 be pleased.
The sacrifice acceptable to God is
 a broken spirit;
 a broken and contrite heart, O
 God, you will not despise.

Do good to Zion in your good
 pleasure;
 rebuild the walls of Jerusalem,
then you will delight in right
 sacrifices,
 in burnt offerings and whole
 burnt offerings;
 then bulls will be offered on
 your altar.

Glory to the Father, and to the
 Son, and to the Holy Spirit:
as it was in the beginning, is now,
 and will be for ever. Amen.

Psalm Prayer

Father, you sent your sinless Son
to save us and bring us back to
you. Ease the stress we feel on
our troubled hearts and help us
to find our way back to you.

Psalm Antiphon

Deliver me from bloodshed, God
of my salvation.

Scripture Reading

Yet we know that a person is justi-
fied not by the works of the law
but through faith in Jesus Christ.
And we have come to believe in
Christ Jesus, so that we might be
justified by faith in Christ, and
not by doing the works of the
law, because no one will be justi-
fied by the works of the law. . . .
For through the law I died to the
law, so that I might live to God.
I have been crucified with Christ;
and it is no longer I who live, but
it is Christ who lives in me. And
the life I now live in the flesh I
live by faith in the Son of God,
who loved me and gave himself
for me.

(GALATIANS 2:16,19–20)

Prayer Response to the Reading

- To you, my Lord, I make my prayer for mercy.
- Hear me, I have sinned against you. I make my prayer for mercy.
- Glory to the Father, and to the Son, and to the Holy Spirit.
- To you, my Lord, I make my prayer for mercy.

Gospel Antiphon

Give your people knowledge of salvation and forgive our sins.

Gospel Canticle

- If you are praying in the morning, pray the morning canticle found on page 249.
- If you are praying in the evening, pray the evening canticle found on page 250.

Glory to the Father, and to the Son, and to the Holy Spirit:.
as it was in the beginning, is now, and will be for ever. Amen.

Gospel Antiphon

Give your people knowledge of salvation and forgive our sins.

Petitions

Our mighty Savior is the source of all hope for those who know the power of his name. Humbly, we pray: *Have mercy and hear our prayer.*

- Renew your holy Church and help its leaders and members walk in the light of hope, we pray. *Have mercy and hear our prayer.*
- Give world leaders the foresight to make decisions that will benefit all of your people, we pray. *Have mercy and hear our prayer.*
- Do not judge us by the wrongs we have done but by the good we long for in our hearts, we pray. *Have mercy and hear our prayer.*
- Show your compassionate love to those who are oppressed and in danger and give them safety and peace, we pray. *Have mercy and hear our prayer.*
- Use us to spread your mercy and hope to those we meet, we pray. *Have mercy and hear our prayer.*

- Give pardon and peace to those who have died and place them with your saints in Heaven, we pray. *Have mercy and hear our prayer.*

Please take time to add your own needs and concerns.

Lord's Prayer

Let us pray in the perfect words taught to us by Jesus:
Our Father . . .

Closing Prayer

Eternal Father, without you we can do nothing. Help our selfishness die and help us live a new life with Jesus at the center. We ask this in his name, in unity with the Holy Spirit. Amen.

Dismissal

May the Lord bless us and protect us from evil and bring us to the joy of Heaven. Amen.

Saturday, Week 4

Call to Prayer

God, come to my assistance.
Lord, make haste to help me.
Glory to the Father, and to the
 Son, and to the Holy Spirit:
as it was in the beginning, is now,
 and will be for ever. Amen.

Psalm Antiphon

Blessed are you, Mary ever virgin,
for you carried the eternal Word
of God in your womb.

Psalm 115

Not to us, O LORD, not to us,
 but to your name give glory,
 for the sake of your steadfast
 love and your faithfulness.
Why should the nations say,
 "Where is their God?"

Our God is in the heavens;
 he does whatever he pleases.
Their idols are silver and gold,
 the work of human hands.
They have mouths, but do not
 speak;
 eyes, but do not see.
They have ears, but do not hear;
 noses, but do not smell.
They have hands, but do not feel;
 feet, but do not walk;

they make no sound in their
 throats.
Those who make them are
 like them;
 so are all who trust in them.

O Israel, trust in the LORD!
 He is their help and their shield.
O house of Aaron, trust in the
 LORD!
 He is their help and their shield.
You who fear the LORD, trust in
 the LORD!
 He is their help and their shield.

The LORD has been mindful
 of us; he will bless us;
 he will bless the house
 of Israel;
 he will bless the house
 of Aaron;
he will bless those who fear
 the LORD,
 both small and great.

May the LORD give you increase,
 both you and your children.
May you be blessed by the LORD,
 who made heaven and earth.

The heavens are the LORD's
 heavens,
 but the earth he has given to
 human beings.

The dead do not praise the LORD,
 nor do any that go down into
 silence.
But we will bless the LORD
 from this time on and
 forevermore.
Praise the LORD!

Glory to the Father, and to the
 Son, and to the Holy Spirit:
as it was in the beginning, is now,
 and will be for ever. Amen.

Psalm Prayer

The Virgin Mary blessed your name, mighty Lord, by her willingness to do what you asked of her. May we bless your name by doing all that you ask us to do.

Psalm Antiphon

Blessed are you, Mary ever virgin, for you carried the eternal Word of God in your womb.

Scripture Reading

For those whom he foreknew he also predestined to be conformed to the image of his Son, in order that he might be the firstborn within a large family. And those whom he predestined he also called; and those whom he called

he also justified; and those whom he justified he also glorified.

(ROMANS 8:29–30)

Prayer Response to the Reading

- We share in the fruit of life through you, chosen daughter blessed by the Lord.
- You humbly accepted your role in the divine plan, chosen daughter blessed by the Lord.
- Glory to the Father, and to the Son, and to the Holy Spirit.
- We share in the fruit of life through you, chosen daughter blessed by the Lord.

Gospel Antiphon

I am the servant of the Lord. Let it be done according to your will.

Gospel Canticle

- If you are praying in the morning, pray the morning canticle found on page 249.
- If you are praying in the evening, pray the evening canticle found on page 250.

Glory to the Father, and to the
 Son, and to the Holy Spirit:

as it was in the beginning, is now, and will be for ever. Amen.

Gospel Antiphon

I am the servant of the Lord. Let it be done according to your will.

Petitions

Jesus, our Savior, chose to come into the world through the Virgin Mary and set her apart for all time. Knowing this to be true, we pray: *May your Mother intercede for us, Lord.*

- Mary answered the angel's call with a humble and sincere heart. Help the Church on earth to follow her timeless example and listen when you call, we pray. *May your Mother intercede for us, Lord.*

- With the help of Joseph, Mary raised you in a loving and holy family. May families today work to become more holy and loving, we pray. *May your Mother intercede for us, Lord.*

- Mary walked with you on the road to Calvary and suffered with you at the foot of your Cross. Help us to endure our own pain and anguish with the same resolve and grace, we pray. *May your Mother intercede for us, Lord.*

- After your death, the disciple whom you loved took in Mary. May we take care of those around us in our own families who are in need, we pray. *May your Mother intercede for us, Lord.*

- You gave Mary as a mother to your disciple and to us. Help us live lives worthy of such a noble and holy woman, we pray. *May your Mother intercede for us, Lord.*

- Mary sits as Queen of Heaven, ready to greet those who have gone before us in faith. May they see her face and all the saints at the heavenly banquet, we pray. *May your Mother intercede for us, Lord.*

Please take time to add your own needs and concerns.

Lord's Prayer

Let us pray in the perfect words taught to us by Jesus:
Our Father . . .

Closing Prayer

Heavenly Father, you take the common and make it uncommon. By coming to your people through the Blessed Virgin Mary, you set her apart from all others, and the child she bore was the Savior of us all. May the common actions of our lives become uncommon and special by your grace and our faith in your love. We ask this in the name of Jesus, the Lord, in unity with the Holy Spirit. Amen.

Dismissal

May the Lord bless us and protect us from evil and bring us to the joy of Heaven. Amen.

Morning Canticle

The Canticle of Zechariah: Luke 1:68–79

Blessed be the Lord, the God
of Israel;
he has come to his people and set
them free.

He has raised up for us a mighty
savior,
born of the house of his servant
David.

Through his holy prophets he
promised of old
that he would save us from our
enemies,
from the hands of all who hate us.

He promised to show mercy to
our fathers
and to remember his holy covenant.

This was the oath he swore to
our father Abraham:
to set us free from the hands of
our enemies,
free to worship him without fear,
holy and righteous in his sight
all the days of our life.

You, my child, shall be called the
prophet of the Most High;
for you will go before the Lord to
prepare his way,

to give his people knowledge
of salvation
by the forgiveness of their sins.

In the tender compassion of
our God
the dawn from on high shall
break upon us,
to shine on those who dwell in
darkness and the shadow
of death,
and to guide our feet into the
way of peace.

Glory to the Father, and to the
Son, and to the Holy Spirit:
as it was in the beginning, is now,
and will be for ever. Amen.

Evening Canticle

The Canticle of Mary
Magnificat:
Luke 1:46–55

My soul proclaims the greatness
of the Lord,
my spirit rejoices in God my
Savior
for he has looked with favor on
his lowly servant.

From this day all generations will
call me blessed:
the Almighty has done great
things for me,
and holy is his Name.

He has mercy on those who
fear him
in every generation.

He has shown the strength of
his arm,
he has scattered the proud in
their conceit.

He has cast down the mighty
from their thrones,
and has lifted up the lowly.

He has filled the hungry with
good things,
and the rich he has sent away
empty.

He has come to the help of his
servant Israel
for he has remembered his
promise of mercy,
the promise he made to our
fathers,
to Abraham and his children
for ever.

Glory to the Father, and to the
Son, and to the Holy Spirit:
as it was in the beginning, is now,
and will be for ever. Amen.

Index

Acknowledgments

The Scripture texts used in the Psalter on pages 160–248 are from the New Revised Standard Version of the Bible, Catholic Edition. Copyright © 1993 and 1989 by the Division of Christian Education of the National Council of the Churches of Christ in the United States of America. All rights reserved.

All other Scripture texts are from the *New American Bible, revised edition* © 2010, 1991, 1986, 1970 Confraternity of Christian Doctrine, Inc., Washington, D.C. All Rights Reserved. No part of this work may be reproduced or transmitted in any form or by any means, electronic or mechanical, including photocopying, recording, or by any information storage and retrieval system, without permission in writing from the copyright owner.

The prayers, devotions, beliefs, and practices contained herein have been verified against authoritative sources.

The material labeled *Catechism* is from the English translation of the *Catechism of the Catholic Church* for use in the United States of America, second edition. Copyright © 1994 by the United States Catholic Conference, Inc.—Libreria Editrice Vaticana (LEV). English transition of the *Catechism of the Catholic Church: Modifications from the Editio Typica* copyright © 1997 by the United States Catholic Conference, Inc.—LEV.

The excerpt on page 33 is from *Liturgical Music Today: A Statement of the Bishops' Committee on the Liturgy on the Occasion of the Tenth Anniversary of Music in Catholic Worship*, by the United States Conference of Catholic Bishops (USCCB) (Washington, DC: USCCB, 1982), page 23. Copyright © 1982 USCCB, Washington, D.C. Used with permission of the USCCB.

The "Blessing for Those Going on a Pilgrimage" on page 43, the "Blessing for One Celebrating a Birthday" and the "Blessing for One

Celebrating an Engagement" on page 45, the "Blessing at a Gravesite" and the "Blessing of a Pet" on page 46, the "Blessing of a Planting," the "Blessing of a Harvest," and the "Blessing of an Advent Wreath" on page 48 are from the English translation of *Book of Blessings* © 1987, International Commission on English in the Liturgy Corporation (ICEL), numbers 603, 343, 211, 1749, 957, 1021, 1021, and 1540, respectively. (Collegeville, MN: Liturgical Press, 1989). Copyright © 1989 by the Order of St. Benedict, Collegeville, MN. All rights reserved. Used with permission of the ICEL and the Bishops' Committee on Divine Worship (BCDW).

The prayer on page 60 is from *Lectionary for [Sunday] Mass: For Use in the Dioceses of the United States of America*, second typical edition, volume I, by the USCCB (Collegeville, MN: Liturgical Press, 1998), page 482. Copyright © 1998 by the Order of St. Benedict, Collegeville, MN. All rights reserved. Used with permission of the USCCB.

The "Confirmation Consecratory Prayer" on page 61 and the "Give the Spirit to Your People" prayer on page 66 are from the English translation of *Rite of Confirmation* (Second Edition), © 1975 ICEL, numbers 42 and 30, in *The Rites of the Catholic Church*, volume one, prepared by the ICEL, a Joint Commission of Catholic Bishops' Conferences (Collegeville, MN: Liturgical Press, 1990). Copyright © 1990 by the Order of St. Benedict, Collegeville, MN. All rights reserved. Used with permission of the ICEL and the BCDW.

The prayers from the Mass on pages 65, 79–80, and 151 are from the English translation of *The Roman Missal* © 2010, ICEL (Washington, DC: USCCB, 2011), pages 1341, 451, 528, 527, 527, 665, and 667, respectively. Copyright © 2011, USCCB, Washington, D.C. All rights reserved. No part of this work may be reproduced or transmitted in any form or by any means, electronic or mechanical, including photocopying, recording, or by any information storage and retrieval system, without permission in writing from the copyright holder. Used with permission of the ICEL and the BCDW.

The prayer by Saint Alphonsus Liguori on page 71; the prayer by Saint Francis de Sales on page 73; the prayer by Saint Catherine of

Siena on page 73; the three prayers by Saint Ignatius of Loyola on pages
73–74; the prayer by Saint Gertrude the Great on page 74; and the
prayer by Saint Augustine of Hippo on page 76 are from The Feast of
All Saints Web site, at *feastofsaints.com/prayersofsaints.htm*.

The devotion on pages 85–88 is from *Manual of Prayers*, Pontifical
North American College, compiled by James D. Watkins (Chicago: Mid-
west Theological Forum; Princeton, NJ: Pontifical North American Col-
lege, 1996), pages 162–167. Copyright © 1996 The American College of
the Roman Catholic Church in the United States. Used with permission
of Midwest Theological Forum.

The quotation and prayer on page 89 are from *The Icon: Window on
the Kingdom*, by Michael Quenot (Crestwood, NY: Saint Vladimir's Sem-
inary Press, 1991), pages 12 and 13. Copyright © 1991 by Saint Vladi-
mir's Seminary Press. Used with permission of Saint Vladimir's Seminary.

The prayer "The Road Ahead" on page 93 is from *Thoughts in
Solitude*, by Thomas Merton (New York: Farrar, Straus, Cudahy, 1956,
1986), page 83. Copyright © 1958 by the Abbey of Our Lady of Geth-
semani. Copyright renewed 1986 by the trustees of the Thomas Merton
Legacy Trust. Used with permission of Farrar, Straus and Giroux, LLC.

The words of Saint Josephine Bakhita on page 98 are from "Black Cath-
olics: Josephine Bakhita," National Black Catholic Congress Web site, at
www.nbccongress.org/black-catholics/black-saints-saint-josephinebakhita.asp.

The prayers "Light a Holy Fire" and "Father, Thank You" on page
100 are reprinted from *An African Prayer Book*, selected by Desmond
Tutu (New York: Walker and Company, 1995), pages 128 and 65–66.
Copyright © 1995 by Desmond Tutu.

The prayers on pages 102–104 and 107–108 are from *Prayer With-
out Borders: Celebrating Global Wisdom*, edited by Barbara Ballenger
(Baltimore, MD: Catholic Relief Services, 2004), pages 101, 49, 29,
31, 47, and 93, respectively. Copyright © by Catholic Relief Services.
Used with permission of Catholic Relief Services.

"The Wayfarer's Prayer" on page 102 is from *Companion of Hopes:
Prayers for Migrant Youth*, by the Youth and Migration Program of the

Mexican Episcopal Commission of Youth Ministry, as quoted in *Prayer Without Borders: Celebrating Global Wisdom*, page 51.

The prayer by Dom Helder Camara on page 103 is reprinted from *Prayer Without Borders: Celebrating Global Wisdom*, pages 44–45. Copyright © by Dom Helder Camara Institute.

"We Pray This Day" on page 107 is from *Kneeling in Jerusalem*, by Ann Weems (Louisville, KY: Westminster/John Knox Press, 1992), page 40. Copyright © 1992 Ann Barr Weems. Used with permission of Westminster John Knox Press.

The section "Praying as a Poem" on pages 111–112 is from the *Teaching Activities Manual for "The Catholic Youth Prayer Book,"* by Rebecca Rushing (Winona, MN: Saint Mary's Press, 2006), handout 8–B. Copyright © 2006 by Saint Mary's Press. All rights reserved.

The section "The Four R's of *Lectio Divina*" on pages 119, 121, and 123–124 is adapted from *Catechetical Sessions on Christian Prayer*, by Laurie Delgatto and Mary Shrader (Winona, MN: Saint Mary's Press, 2004), pages 95–96. Copyright © 2004 by Saint Mary's Press. All rights reserved.

The guided meditation on pages 130 and 132 is adapted from "Baptism: This Is My Beloved Child," in the leader's guide for *Guided Meditations for Youth on Sacramental Life*, by Jane E. Arsenault and Jean R. Cedor (Winona, MN: Saint Mary's Press, 1993), pages 11–17. Copyright © 1993 by Saint Mary's Press. All rights reserved.

The "Prayer and Journaling" chapter on pages 135–142 and the "Personal Salvation History" sidebar on page 136 are adapted from *PrayerWays*, by Carl Koch (Winona, MN: Saint Mary's Press, 1995), pages 91–93 and 94. Copyright © 1995 by Saint Mary's Press. All rights reserved.

The excerpts and quotation by Pope John Paul II on pages 149, 152, and 153 are from *Constitution on the Sacred Liturgy* (*Sacrosanctum Concilium*, 1963), numbers 11, 48, and 2, respectively, at *www.vatican.va/archive/hist_councils/ ii_vatican_council/documents/vat-ii_const_19631204_sacrosanctum-concilium_en.html*. Copyright © LEV.

The "Canticle of Zechariah" and the "Canticle of Mary" on pages 249–250 are from the English translation by the International Consultation on English Texts, and reprinted here from the English translation of *The Liturgy of the Hours*, ICEL (New York: Catholic Book Publishing, 1975), volume III, pages 656–657 and 669–670. Copyright © 1975 Catholic Book Publishing.

The "Call to Prayer" sections in chapter 16 are from the English translation of *The Liturgy of the Hours* © 1970, 1973, 1975, ICEL (New York: Catholic Book Publishing, 1975), volume III, page 651. Copyright © 1975 Catholic Book Publishing. Used with permission of the ICEL and the BCDW.

To view copyright terms and conditions for Internet materials cited here, log on to the home pages for the referenced Web sites.

During this book's preparation, all citations, facts, figures, names, addresses, telephone numbers, Internet URLs, and other pieces of information cited within were verified for accuracy. The authors and Saint Mary's Press staff have made every attempt to reference current and valid sources, but we cannot guarantee the content of any source, and we are not responsible for any changes that may have occurred since our verification. If you find an error in, or have a question or concern about, any of the information or sources listed within, please contact Saint Mary's Press.

Endnotes Cited in Quotations from the *Catechism of the Catholic Church*, Second Edition

1. Cf. *Romans* 8:29; Council of Trent (1547): Denzinger-Schönmetzer, *Enchiridion Symbolorum, definitionum et declarationum de rebus fidei et morum* (1965) 1609–1619.

2. *Sacrosanctum concilium* 84; *1 Thessalonians* 5:17; *Ephesians* 6:18.

Notes